The
Maubrey
Destined
Effect

The Journey to The Kingdom of Heaven

Vol. II

By

Maubrey Destined

DPH

Destined Publishing House
8549 Wilshire Blvd. #750
Beverly Hills, CA 90211

To invest in the Maubrey Destined brand, or for more information about special discounts for bulk purchases, please contact Destined Publishing House Special Sales And Investments at Investments@MaubreyDestined.com

CONTENTS

PRELUDE

Before one can compose the greatest, most motivational, and inspiring literary masterpiece of all time, one must live the greatest, most motivational and inspiring life. One must also read the greatest, most motivational and inspiring literary masterpiece of all time, from front to back, with an open, humble, and believing heart – The Holy Bible!
-Maubrey Destined

"Whatever you do, you have to make sure that you always set yourself up." he said. Meaning, always make sure that the actions that you are taking, or will be taking, will produce the results that you are desiring and hoping for. Such a simple piece of advice, but I have remembered and utilized it to this day, almost a decade later. I believe that meeting Luke Jones was a divine connection.

It was a lot of strenuous work during those hot summer days, but overall, I had a good time. I bonded with the other construction workers. I had to do work that I had never known how to do before. I used to get on a big, Russian guy's nerves that worked for Luke's company. It was so funny to me. He had a quick temper, and would get upset, with his deep Russian accent, whenever I didn't move fast enough, or whenever I wasn't strong enough to perform some tasks.

We had many laughs though. All the workers had love for me. The Mexican workers were also funny. We used to make so many jokes while we were working to let the time under the hot summer sun pass by. We were always laughing. They all knew how excited I was to go to Indiana. All throughout the day, someone would shout out, "Indiana!" And then we would all start laughing out loud. None of us could imagine what kind of place Indiana was. They were all excited for me.

The last couple of days were the hardest. I had no idea that I would have gotten attached to these great guys that I had only known for a few weeks. Each worker had their own unique funny personality. They really made my final days in New Jersey enjoyable.

Yet again, it was time to journey forward. What new obstacles and adventures lay before me, I had no idea. Now, there was first, being born in Germany, and moving after only two years. There was, having lived in Africa, then leaving in just three years. Then, we lived in the basement apartment for some time, and then moved again. Next, there was the second floor apartment that we lived in, for just two years, until we moved to New Jersey. Again, there was attending Madison Avenue School for less than one and a half school years. Then, just as I began to get comfortable, and started making friends at Madison Avenue School, it was, once again, time for me to move forward to Union Avenue School. Just a year later, I was transferred to Thurgood Marshall School. Next, after only one year at Thurgood Marshall School, it was time for me to relocate again, back to the newly built Union Avenue School. After rebelling, and getting myself expelled just a year later, I was off to Myrtle Avenue School. Less than a year later, I graduated and journeyed through high school for four years, the longest time period I had stayed in one location throughout the course of my life. Now, The Lord was directing me to Indiana University-Bloomington!

That was the year that the long time, legendary Indiana University basketball coach, Bobby Knight, was fired for grabbing a student by the neck. Bobby Knight's firing made national headlines, including the cover of Sports Illustrated magazine, and was covered on all the major media outlets. Thousands of Indiana University students protested, including star basketball players, who threatened to quit the team if Bobby Knight wasn't allowed to continue coaching. The story sounded quite familiar to what had happened in my high school to my wrestling coach.

I remember sitting in front of the television in my living room at home in Irvington, New Jersey, just amazed that I was soon going to be in that very school. That was also the year when star football player, Antwaan Randle El was one of the top candidates to receive the Heisman Trophy, the award given to the best college football player in the nation. The Indiana University wrestling and soccer teams were both top ranked in the country. The Indiana University business school was ranked highly in the country. The school of music had previously been ranked #1 in the country tied with Juilliard and Eastman School of Music. The school was rated one of the most beautiful campuses in the country, and Playboy magazine ranked Indiana University the college with most beautiful women in the country. Needless to say, I was a happy young man! It was an exciting period, and I couldn't wait to go!

Days later, my bags were packed, and I found myself at the airport hugging my proud parents – my mom, teary eyed, as I kissed her good-bye. I remember being on the plane so nervous and excited at the same time. I envisioned my future ahead of me. I couldn't believe it. I was actually doing this! It was really happening!

The moment I landed in Indiana and stepped out of the plane that night, I stepped into a new dimension! I took a deep breath of the fresh Indiana air into my lungs. I felt the cool, crisp evening air rub against my skin as I walked to the shuttle van that would take me to my new campus in Bloomington.

I took the shuttle from Indianapolis airport to the Indiana University campus in Bloomington, Indiana, about an hour north. In my mind, we couldn't get there fast enough. I was fascinated and intrigued by this new land called Indiana. Wide-eyed, I gazed out of the window, trying to capture every single site that I was seeing. I was fascinated! We drove through miles of cornfields and saw many farm animals and old rustic barns, until the long, tiresome journey of the flight had finally caught up to me. Sitting there in my seat, I slowly drifted into a deep sleep.

After about an hour on the road, late at night, I awoke to the sound of the shuttle van driver alerting us that we were but five minutes away from campus. I rubbed my eyes, smiled, stretched my arms, and took a deep yawn as I braced myself. My heart filled with endless joy and anticipation.

Finally, the shuttle van dropped us off at the Indiana University campus hotel, called the Union.

"Here we are..." the van driver announced.

I stood up and exited the van, taking my first steps onto the land of Bloomington. I had finally arrived! The hotel and the surroundings were just so beautiful! The driver gave me my luggage, I tipped him, and then, I was off into the mezzanine of the hotel with my luggage and brand new bike that I had actually brought with me on the plane, all the way from New Jersey.

In complete euphoria, I immediately phoned home and told them that I had arrived safely, describing to my parents how absolutely beautiful the campus was.

Next, I walked over to the yellow book telephone directory and called the number of the first local taxi cab company that I could find. As I waited, I quickly made friends with a nice Asian girl. We talked about where we were from. We talked about our lives, our goals, and what subject we would be majoring in during that year. I believe she told me that she was going into her sophomore or junior year at Indiana University.

After some time had passed, her taxi cab arrived. Mine had taken quite some time, being that I had called for a taxi cab before her. As the taxi cab driver loaded her luggage into the trunk, she suggested that we share a cab, since her condominium apartment on campus was only a few minutes away from the dormitory building that I would be living in.

"Sure." I replied.

It would save the both of us a few dollars. I helped load her luggage into the cab, and we were on our way. After a few minutes on the road, we arrived in front of my dormitory building, Eigenmenn Hall. It makes me feel good just to say the name, 'Eigenmenn Hall'. This is what a true college experience should feel like. This is how you should feel while reminiscing the journey!

"It looks like no one is in the lobby." the taxi driver said, "I think they are closed for the night."

I exited the taxi cab and went into the lobby to make sure. He was right. My heart sank. I contemplated having to sleep on the floor of the cold lobby until the staff came in to work the next morning during the official check-in day. I couldn't afford to spend the little money that I had on the luxury Indiana Union building's hotel. For a second, I pondered what to do. Just as I started to think, the pretty Asian girl generously offered to let me spend the night over at her apartment until I could check-in in the morning. Immediately, I thought to myself, "Oh boy!"

The look of the taxi cab driver's face was of even more shock and slyness than mine was. I thought about all the college sex stories that I had been hearing about and watching on television, for the past few years. I hadn't been in college for more than an hour, and already, I was going to be spending the night at a random, cute, Asian girl's apartment. It felt like a scene from a movie. Was this a preview of how my college life was going to be? I thought I had died and gone to Heaven!

I must say, I was very surprised and caught off guard by her kind offer. The thought of a stranger that I had just met, less than an hour before, offering their home to me was inconceivable up until that point. In the dangerous and untrusting environment that I was from, you could not even fathom of making such an offer without the fear that the person would rob or harm you once you are alone with them. I must say, my heart was touched by her offer. She showed me a new type of person that I had never known existed. I graciously accepted her offer and re-entered the taxi cab.

After a short drive, we arrived in front of my new friend's condominium apartment. I helped the driver get our luggage out of the trunk, and then I covered the cab fee. It was the least I could do, to repay her for her kindness.

Meanwhile, I had no idea what to expect after we entered her apartment. I remember telling myself to just go with the flow of whatever happens. I wondered if, after all this time, I would lose my virginity on my first night in college. It wasn't exactly how I had envisioned it to happen, but I was prepared for anything.

As the cab drove away, she walked upstairs to open her apartment door with her keys. I carried our heavy luggage one by one up the stairs. With a smile on my face, I walked in to a very nice, lovely scented one bedroom apartment and shut the door.

Welcome to college!

The Maubrey Destined *Effect*

The Journey to The Kingdom of Heaven

Vol. II

May this book move, inspire, and motivate you to higher levels that you have never even fathomed. May this book reveal the secrets of unlocking all of your hidden gifts and finally obtaining absolute and total happiness!

Chapter 1

The Asian girl's condo reminded me of my cousin Hannah's condo that I stayed in when I visited her in Tallahassee, Florida. That's pretty much where the excitement and anticipation came to an end. I wish I could say that she cut out the lights, and we had passionate sex all night long, just like I had seen in the movies. But the truth is that she told me that I could sleep on her futon sofa in her living room.

I remember telling my new friends that I had made a few days later the entire story about me meeting a beautiful Asian girl my first day on campus and being invited to sleep in her apartment after finding out that my dormitory was closed. But instead of telling them that I had spent the entire night sleeping on the futon, I told them that she first told me that I could sleep on the futon, then a few minutes later, after I began to fall asleep, she came out of her room with nothing but a thong on and a glass of water, asking me if I wanted a drink, with a seductive smile on her face. I told my new friends that I smiled and said, "Yeah...! Definitely...!"

You could tell that I have a great imagination. I told my friends that we first had sex on her futon, and then, I carried her to her room and had sex on her bed all night long.

I must have told that fantasy story over a dozen times. And each time I told it, my friends' jaws would drop with excitement. If I had only known that there was no need to fabricate that story, that I would experience much more outrageous, wild and unbelievable stories very soon.

I awoke the next morning to the most beautiful day that I had ever realized. I had the warmth of the sun shining on my face, through the window shades. It was a surreal feeling. Just 24 hours earlier, I woke up in a poor town of Irvington, New Jersey. But now, I was in the beautiful Bloomington, Indiana! And I was here to stay! It was a wonderful feeling to know that overnight, my life had drastically changed for the better.

It finally hit me, of what I had been working so hard for all my life. But I knew that if I wanted to stay in this newly discovered paradise, then I would have to get focused and work very hard.

I called home and spoke to my parents for a while. They were so happy and excited for me.

Soon afterwards, the Asian girl woke up, and we ate a light breakfast together. She then gave me her contact number to keep in touch. I assembled my mountain bike, thanked her for her kind hospitality, gave her a hug, promising to stay in touch, and was out the door and on my way to Eigenmenn Hall dormitory to start my new life as a college student!

I didn't want to spend the limited money that I had to call for a taxi cab to drive me to my dormitory that was only five minutes away. So, I saddled my brand new, blue and white mountain bike, and with my left hand on the bike handle, and my right hand holding the handle of my suitcase, I began to pedal my way down the sides of the winding campus streets.

I remember passing a post office and highly trafficked streets filled with freshmen, returning students, and their families. I pedaled for about a mile and a half, my suitcase in hand, rolling down the street, as I tried to balance myself up and down hills, between cars, and under narrow bridge passages – all under the hot summer's August heat.

I could only imagine what the people in traffic were thinking. It was truly a comical site to see.

As I write, I must pause, because of the flashbacks that I'm getting of my current ex-girlfriend, the love of my life that just broke up with me less than two weeks ago. It's crazy and ironic to think about it. By this time, I would usually be showering, dressing up, and getting ready to go spend the entire weekend at her apartment in the Upper West Side of Manhattan. The long and endless two hour journey I would take to see my love never mattered the least bit, as long as I was able to see my heart… But I must digress for now. I shall explain later on, toward the end of my story.

For now, on my first day as a 17 year old freshman in Indiana University - Bloomington, both our worlds are light-years apart. Our hearts are yet to collide. My love and I have never met. She is but a 12 year old child in Haiti. I am nowhere in her thoughts… Or am I…? It would be quite many years before our paths would cross. Proceeding, I finally arrived and checked into Eigenmenn Hall.

"Hi, welcome to IU. What's your name please?" the girl behind the front desk nicely asked.

"Maubrey Okoe-Quansah." I answered with a big smile on my face.

"There you are…!" she replied.

19

She found my name on the student list. She gave me my room and mailbox key, then I made my way to the elevator, excited than ever to see my new eighth floor, single bedroom that I would be spending the year in. That elevator ride up was symbolic of the direction where my life was headed. I recall the elevator ride vividly. I was wearing a baby blue Gap tank top, revealing my muscles. I was wearing khaki, three-quarter shorts, and brown leather, Lord and Taylor open toe sandals. I had my nice clothes on, feeling confident about my brand new life! I remember sparking a conversation with my next door, floormate and his family. We were all so excited. It was a happy time. Everyone was so nice. They all smiled and said hi to me when they passed me. I had never been around such friendly and cheerful people. These were my kind of people.

I had finally reached my small one bedroom. I opened the door, brought my luggage inside, shut the door behind me, and took a moment of silence to myself.

"I'm really here…! This is really happening…!"

.The room was small and cozy, with just enough space for an extended twin bed, a desk and chair, a drawer, and some walking room. But I loved the eighth floor view from my room.

I unpacked as much as I could that morning, then went out into the hallway to meet the rest of the floormates, including my next door neighbor, an Indian kid named William, who ended up becoming one of my best friends.

Later, I decided to take a bike ride alone through campus. The minute I laid my eyes on the Indiana University campus, I was in love! My eyes were exposed to such beautiful scenery that I had never seen before. The lawns were perfectly manicured. All I saw were the most beautiful collegiate gothic limestone buildings everywhere I went. As I rode deeper into the campus, I discovered hidden bike trails and flowing streams. There were the most lovely sycamore trees that I don't recall ever seeing before. You could see tall evergreen trees and colorful and vibrant flower beds everywhere. In other areas, you could find graceful arches, glistening ponds, and sprawling fields. The campus was truly heaven on earth for me. I could not imagine being anywhere else in the world at that moment, but in Indiana University. God had really outdone Himself in the favor that He was showing me, and really caused me to make one of the best decisions in my life in choosing to go to Indiana University. And anyone who has spent more than a day on the Indiana University campus will tell you that you can't talk about the Indiana University campus without talking about the most amazing, cutest, friendly, squirrels in the world that live there. Yes, squirrels. They are everywhere on campus. You could be walking to class, and there they would be, in the middle of the walkway, without a care in the world, usually standing on their hind legs, just snacking on an acorn. They don't even bother moving out of your way in fear. The squirrels usually just stand there, minding their business and enjoying their daily snack, as you courteously walk around them. I had never seen anything like that before in my life. It was literally, squirrel-topia (if that's a real word). They had all the acorns in the world on that campus. All the squirrels were chubby. I absolutely loved those cute, chubby brown squirrels. They often made my day.

As I continued to ride, my eyes were exposed to a variety of lovely natural colors. You could see vivid purples, blues, lavenders, and violets. You could see radiant reds, pinks, oranges, whites, and golden browns. You could see romantic gazebos. There were lounges and benches, wonderfully sculpted statues made out of pure limestone, and lush designs throughout campus.

The campus was graceful. It was aesthetically wonderful! The picturesque landscaped was utterly an architectural masterpiece! Whoever the masterminds of designing the campus are, they are true artistic geniuses.

During the first week of school, I got straight to business. I called the wrestling and football coaches' offices to find out practice times. Unfortunately, I was told that it was too late for me to join the football team, since they had been practicing since mid summer. But I managed to find out when the wrestling team had their practices. I wasn't recruited by the team while I was in high school, but I didn't care. I knew that I had talent, and I was going to walk-on to the team. My plan was to wrestle that year, and then wrestle and play football each year afterwards.

I wanted to be a doctor, so I enrolled in all pre-med classes. As always, I had very ambitious goals. I was mentally prepared to study and work harder than I ever had in my life, in order to achieve all my dreams. I had everything planned out. My future looked very promising.

But then, about a week after being on campus, I received a letter in the mail from the bursar's office, the department of the university that handles students' tuition payments. It said that my balance of roughly $12,000 dollars, for the first semester, was due soon! My heart dropped to the floor! I panicked. I couldn't believe what I was reading. I hoped it was a mistake.

Back in New Jersey, about a few weeks after being accepted to Indiana University, I received an ambiguous letter in the mail from the university that made it seem that I had received grants and academic scholarships, and that my parents only had to pay about $2000 dollars per semester. I remember that night clearly. After opening the letter and reading it for a second and third time, my heart pounding with joy, I remember running to my parents in the kitchen and telling them the great news. We felt that The Lord Jesus had answered our prayers.

After receiving the acceptance letter in the mail, I had made up my mind that I was going to Indiana University, regardless of whether I received a scholarship, a grant, or financial aid. My parents never set up a college savings plan while we were growing up. But the idea of how I was going to pay for Indiana University once I arrived there didn't even enter my mind. But now that I was under the impression that I had received about 90% of my tuition fees in financial aid, scholarships and grants, it was an extra blessing. I assumed that my 3.3 grade point average, my 1190 SAT score, and my athletic achievements were enough to earn the generous financial aid. Apparently, I was wrong. I could see my mom and me in our kitchen now, as we jubilantly jumped up and down hugging and kissing each other, and shouting in celebration. It was such a happy night for us.

So, now that I was in Indiana, reading the letter stating that I had to pay a balance of $12,000 dollars, I was very shocked and confused. I called my parents immediately and told them the devastating news. During the conversation they suggested that I return home, and consider going to a local college.

Suddenly, I had awakened from my sweet dream. And now, a dark cloud was hovering above my head. I had a very serious decision to make. I could concede defeat, and pack my bags up and go right back to Irvington, New Jersey to live with my parents. Or I could try and stay, and figure out what to do.

It was an easy decision! There was no way that I was going to go back to the ghetto! I figured that since my room, board, and meals were already included in my balance for the year, that I would be able to survive, at least for that year while I figured out what to do.

I kept moving forward! I continued going to wrestling practice. I went to all my classes on my weekly schedule. I couldn't afford to buy all my books, especially my biology books, which was the subject I was majoring in. Altogether, my book fees totaled about one thousand dollars. My parents only sent me a few hundred dollars, so I could only afford to buy the least expensive books. I remember having to borrow and share biology books with different classmates that lived in my dormitory building. It was very inconvenient for my classmates. And just a few hours a week to use the books were certainly not enough for me to succeed. I was trying the best that I could.

However, it wasn't all work and no play. I worked hard during the week, and when the weekends came around, I partied hard. I was still only 17 years old. There was still another month before I would turn 18 years old, but I was getting into 21 and over night clubs. This was a far stretch from my previous life in Irvington, New Jersey. I would have never dreamed of going out to a night club in Irvington. It was just too dangerous. But here in Bloomington, Indiana, I was in the safest town, surrounded by my wrestling teammates and other college students.

That's when the girls came into the picture! All of a sudden, I went from hardly getting attention from girls in high school to getting constant attention from all kinds of girls in college. I couldn't quite understand where the sudden attention came from. In high school, I was just another guy, but now, I was the object of many beautiful girls' desire. It was a lot to handle in the beginning. I wasn't used to it, but I definitely embraced it all!

The first time I had a girl in my dorm room was within the first few weeks of school. A group of us were standing outside, in front of the dorms one night, when one Polish girl brought up the subject of getting and giving massages. I remember immediately getting turned on and realized that she was flirting with me.

The next thing I know, we are both in our underwear, and I'm on top of her in my room giving her a massage with all the lights off, except a red light bulb. I was just about to finally lose my virginity and have sex with her, when my Indian buddy William, from the next room over, unexpectedly walked in the door. It was a funny site to see. He had a shocked and excited look, with the biggest smile on his face. He quickly apologized for interrupting us and shut the door as he smiled from cheek to cheek.

The mood was gone. We gave each other massages for a few more minutes before she went back upstairs to her dorm room. I was this close to losing my virginity. But for some reason, I wasn't upset at all. Maybe, I had a feeling that there would be many more nights like this on campus.

I remember my next door buddy rushing back into my room as soon as the Polish girl left to find out all the details. We were both so excited. This was my first time giving a girl a massage in my room. Then, it finally happened, just a few days later! But not with the Polish girl who lived upstairs in my dorm building.

I must admit, at this moment, it's getting harder and harder to share my story, because as I am about to write, I am realizing how sensitive, personal and private this topic is to me. Up until this time, I've reserved this part of my life to only about a handful of close friends and family. I've been blessed to have lost my virginity to such a wonderful girl, and I will always hold that sacred experience close to my heart.

There was a girl who lived in the same dorm building as me. She was also in my biology class and was kind enough to let me borrow her biology book to study whenever I needed it. She became a good friend in the few short weeks of school since I met her. She had a younger sister who was a senior in high school, and had come to visit her that night.

I remember my next door buddy, William, who had seen her already, coming to me all excited, and telling me how cute she was. I got excited as well and couldn't wait to see her. I quickly put on some clothes and went upstairs to the girls' floor with my buddy to meet her.

There was instant chemistry. She was a beautiful Vietnamese girl with long, straight hair, smooth skin, catlike eyes, soft pink lips, and thick hips and thighs. We all hung out in her sister's room, casually talking and telling jokes.

Next, we decided to go downstairs to the recreation room of the dormitory. I remember sexual tension growing, as we played a few games of pool. There were lots of laughing and smiling throughout the time.

Then, the girl and I decided to separate from her sister and my buddy, and went to play basketball alone outside on the court. She had no idea, but every passing minute, I was falling deeper and deeper for her. It was an amazing feeling that I had in my chest. I had only met her a few hours before, but there was such an intense attraction between us. I knew she was a special girl. We played basketball and flirted for a little while longer, and then we decided to go to my dorm room.

On the way to my room, I remember being so erect, underneath my black basketball shorts, that I had to pretend that I was scratching my left thigh the entire walk to my dorm room. I remember trying to think of all sorts of things to get my mind off of her, but it was useless. My hormones were at their peak.

We flirted in my room for a while. I had no idea what to do. I was more nervous than I had ever been in my life. Both of us were virgins, but she had no idea that I was a virgin like her. I lied and told her that I had sex a few times already. I didn't want her to know that I was inexperienced and ruin my chance of having sex with her. I could tell that she was nervous too. We both procrastinated and staled, making small talk, not knowing how to go to the next base. Finally, as we were flirting on the bed, she sat right on my lap and looked deep into my eyes with those catlike eyes of hers. She could literally feel my excitement. As she pierced into my eyes, she pressed her soft, sweet lips against mine, causing my heart to start beating at a million miles per hour! I couldn't believe that it was actually happening! Just a few weeks after being in Indiana University, at the tender age of 17 years old, I was about to lose my virginity!

I softly caressed her body and her breasts as I gently laid her on my bed. We continued kissing as we slowly removed each other's clothes. My heart continued to race! I briefly departed from her and turned off the main bedroom lights and put on some music, then reached to my bedside lamp to turn on what I called "the red light special". I climbed back in bed, on top of her, and continued where I had left off.

Soon, we were both bare-skinned, me on top of her, with the sensation of our warm bodies pressed against one another. I proceeded to foreplay, imitating what I had seen on adult movies all those years leading to that night.

Next, I reached under my pillow and pulled out the condom that I had hidden just a few moments earlier, while she wasn't paying attention. I was very sly. Doing that, later on, turned out to be my trademark. She smiled, wondering where the condom had mysteriously come from. She then helped me roll the condom on. I remember taking my time and having extreme pleasure during foreplay, however, I was really trying to figure out how to penetrate into her. I had no idea how to penetrate without looking.

Soon, I think she realized that I was having difficulty navigating her virgin seas. She guided me with her warm, sweaty palms, as she continued to gaze endlessly into my eyes.

Finally, the moment of pure euphoria had arrived! This time, my room door was definitely locked! (I made sure of that). There would be no interruptions from my new best bud next door. I was in! Inch after inch, I slowly and gently slide in and out, between her virgin walls, as she gave a look of pleasure and slight discomfort on her face. After only about a quarter of the way inside her, she could not bare the pain. We rocked back and forth, attempting to penetrate deeper, but there was no change. I was certain that her waters were uncharted. And the fact that I am very well endowed didn't help either. After just a few minutes later, we stopped because of the discomfort she was beginning to feel. We kissed and cuddled ourselves to sleep.

The next morning, we made love again. It lasted a similar amount of time as the night before, but this time, with a little bit more pleasure and comfort. And that's the story of when I lost my virginity.

I had fallen in love with a beautiful Vietnamese girl. As I mentioned earlier, she was a senior in high school, so she had to drive back home the next day. We kept in touch for a couple of months, writing love letters to each other and constantly speaking on the phone. She even drove back to campus to visit me a few times. But after just a couple of months, we lost touch when she realized that I wasn't willing to be monogamous. Being in an exclusive relationship was the last thing on my mind. At that time, I was only focused on my grades, wrestling, and having sex with as many beautiful girls as possible. She was the sweetest girl. She definitely did not deserve that.

It's amazing. As I began to relive the fond memories that I had with her, just a few days ago, I decided to search her name on Facebook. I found her and requested to be her friend. She accepted my friend request within a few minutes. My heart was so happy that after eight long years, she had put the past behind her, and forgiven me for the way that I treated her.

I sent her a message saying, "Awe - I miss you Alexis. Hope you've been well! xo Maubrey".

Two days later, I checked my messages, and to my surprise, she replied to my message. My heart filled with more joy, that the wonderful girl that I lost my virginity to, sent me a message.

To my dismay, she replied, "I'm sorry... I don't remember u... How do I know u?"

Wow! I was shocked and surprised that she didn't recognize me. Had I physically changed that much since my freshman year, that she couldn't recognize the boy who she lost her virginity to?

"Wow...umm...I was your first...I think..." I replied.

"Maybe," I thought, "since she knew me only by my middle name, 'Michael', she is a bit confused."

"Or maybe, she is just joking or pretending, just to make conversation."

I quickly realized the answer to my thoughts in her next message.

"Most definitely not sorry wrong person." she replied.

And as fast as she confirmed me as a friend, she removed me as a friend.

Another valuable lesson learned in this journey that I am on. The actions and behaviors that you have now can have a profound effect on you many years from now. It's important to treat everyone with decency, and to continue living in integrity and righteousness, all the days of your life. I broke her heart a long time ago. It hurts; however, I understand why she would not want to be a friend.

Chapter 2

9/11

It was just the most picture perfect day. I was blissfully riding my blue and white mountain bike through campus, on my way to my dormitory, from my sociology class. I strolled passed the sparkling pond, observing how the sun's rays majestically bounced off the water. You could hear the sound of birds chirping in the background. Squirrels were playing in the grass as usual. The wind was gently blowing in my face as a rode forward. There were a few students here and there, walking and riding their bikes to and from class. All was good. It was a typical day at Indiana University.

Midway to the dorms, I'll never forget what happened next.

A kid shouted to me, "They just bombed the World Trade Center!"

My initial thought was: "Yeah... I know... Like five years ago, when I was in high school."

I imagined that, for some reason, perhaps, because he was probably from Indiana, and not New York like I was, he had just found out about the World Trade Center basement bombing that happened many years before. But he had a frantic look on his face.

"Really!?" I replied.

"Yeah!" he exclaimed. "It's all over the news!"

I immediately thought about my mom. She always took the subway trains to work, through the World Trade Center in the morning. I prayed that she wasn't there during the bomb. I pedaled my bike a little faster to confirm the information with the next person on my route.

"They just blew up the World Trade Center!" another student yelled hysterically.

I stepped on the pedal and went racing to my dorm building as fast as I could! I finally arrived and rushed into the lobby of my dormitory building.

When I entered, there was a somber and horrified look on everyone's face, like they had all just seen a ghost. At that point, I was sure that the World Trade Center had definitely been bombed. I tried to remain calm as I waited patiently in the elevator, on my way up to my room.

There was a crowd of students with their eyes fixed on the television in the study lounge of our floor. I briefly watched for a while, and then proceeded to my room to call home.

I thank God...! My mom was ok! She had gone through the World Trade Center just hours before the attack. Virtually every channel was covering the horrific news. I remember watching images of one of the buildings of the World Trade Center on fire from the plane that had collided into it, when suddenly, out of nowhere, another plane rocketed into the other twin skyscraper. All you saw were thick, black smoke and huge flames of fire, blazing from both buildings.

Moments later, both skyscrapers went tumbling to the ground, killing thousands of innocent civilians. It was a horrible sight to see! Next, the news reported that a third and fourth plane had crashed in Pennsylvania and the Pentagon in Arlington, Virginia. It was soon confirmed that the plane crashes were terrorist attacks. Our country was now at war!

In the following days, there were numerous reports of harassment and verbal abuse against students of color and students who looked like they were from the Middle East. I recall hearing that some students, who were being harassed, had reported the incidents to the school administration and were transferred to a different dormitory building.

During that same time, a few of my wrestling teammates wanted me to move to their dormitory building, which was closer to the stadium where we practiced.

Foster Harper dorms – the majority of the freshman wrestlers lived there. I pretended that someone had written a racial slur on my room door as well. And just days later, I was transferred to Foster Harper dorms, where the majority of the freshman wrestlers and other freshman student athletes lived.

I no longer had a single room to myself as I did in Eigenmenn Hall dormitory. But it was ok. Now, I was able to form a closer bond with my teammates. My new roommate was a huge, almost six and a half foot tall, 400 plus pound kid. At times, I thought he was strange and weird, but overall he was a good guy.

During the weekends, I used to come home from nightclubs, house parties, and fraternity parties at around four in the morning, and tell him all my exciting stories about the beautiful girls that I had been with. He was always slightly upset and irritated that I had awoken him from his sleep, but I could tell that he loved hearing the stories. I could go on for hours, giving him play by play details of my entire night. He was able to live vicariously through me.

The mornings after my nights out were always my favorites. I was able to relive my amazing night with my friends, through my stories. I see now that, that was the beginning of my story-telling talents.

Every week, I would work hard in classes, and then when the weekends came around, I was ready to enjoy myself at parties.

Finally, on October 7, 2001, exactly eight years ago from today, I turned eighteen! I was finally legal! I was no longer considered a child. It was most definitely a liberating day for me. I remember celebrating so much that night with my wrestling teammates. All I remember was people buying me drink after drink, and ending the night dancing in the nude, at about four in the morning, with music blasting on top of one of my teammate's bright yellow pickup truck in front of the Foster Harper dorms. We laughed so hard that night. I definitely was carefree, and knew how to have a good time, especially on my eighteenth birthday! I was very aware of where I was. I felt blessed and fortunate to be where I was, and the direction that I was headed in life, at that age.

Chapter 3

Time was flying by. Soon, it was Thanksgiving holiday break. All the students were flying and driving back home to spend time with their families for the week. I could not afford a flight back home to New Jersey. One of my best friends and teammate, Tyler, who lived near Pittsburgh, Pennsylvania, suggested that I come to spend Thanksgiving with him and his family. There was only one problem though. We had no certain way to get to Pittsburgh. What a crazy adventure we were about to have!

Tyler asked one of his friends who was driving to Ohio, if we could hitch a ride with him. So we drove all the way to Ohio in a tightly packed small car, having no clue how we were going to get to Pittsburgh once we got to Ohio. We were just going to go with the flow and figure it out once we reached Ohio.

When we finally got to Ohio, Tyler's friend, the driver we were hitching the ride with asked us where we wanted him to drop us off. We looked at one another puzzled, with absolutely no idea of what our plans were going to be. Neither Tyler nor I had ever been in Ohio before.

After driving around for quite some time, trying to come up with ideas, we finally decided that he should drop us off at Ohio State University's campus. Tyler's friend, who was driving, seemed pretty confused and baffled that we wanted to be dropped off in the middle of nowhere, on the campus of Ohio State University. We were equally as confused and baffled. He offered us many times, to come spend Thanksgiving with his family. But we humbly declined, assuring him that we would figure out how to get all the way to Pittsburgh, Pennsylvania with hardly any money or any plan in mind. Moments later, we were out of his car unloading our bags. I watched Tyler's friend, as he slowly and hesitantly drove away.

It's amazing. We had no idea what we were going to do, alone that night on the almost deserted Ohio State University campus, but we were both so positive and sure that we were going to figure a way to get all the way to Pittsburgh, Pennsylvania, which was almost 200 miles away.

We lugged our bags into the lobby of the nearest dormitory that we could find. We spoke to everyone around. Fortunately, Tyler was as social, if not, more social than I was. We decided to ask students where the Ohio State freshman wrestlers roomed.

Before long, we were knocking on the door of a few Ohio State wrestlers' dorm room. It must have been the most random and spontaneous thing that I had ever done up to that point.

It was amazing! We told them that we were Indiana University freshman wrestlers ourselves and told them the entire story of how we were trying to get to Pennsylvania for Thanksgiving and needed a place to stay for the night. It was truly amazing how well they embraced and welcomed complete strangers into their dorm rooms. I had never seen anything like it. What they did was pure brotherhood at its peak. Just like our school, their starting varsity wrestling team had traveled to another state for a wrestling tournament, but the freshman wrestlers remained behind with the option of either staying on campus or returning home for the holidays.

The Ohio state freshman wrestlers welcomed us into their dorm rooms and called the other wrestlers and friends in the building to introduce us to them. They even went out and bought cases of beer and vodka to show us a great time. I can't talk highly enough about those great guys. They instantly became our brothers.

Thinking about them now, I get a euphoric feeling of how genuinely kind they were to Tyler and me. We learned so much from each other. I remember Tyler telling me to show them some of my dance moves. Tyler was a great friend. He always praised me and spoke highly of me in front of other people.

Soon, we were drinking, we had good music playing, and we were all dancing my dance that I had taught them. Moments like these are what life is really all about!

After sharing stories, drinking, and celebrating our new found friendship for a few hours, they took us out to a few parties. I remember them introducing me to the most beautiful, exotic, bleach blond haired girl. I had never before seen anything like her! She was simply angelic! We talked off and on, on the route to the different house parties. There was definitely chemistry between the girl and me.

We went from one house party after another. We were having the best time in this newly discovered land. We were at the last house party while I was talking to another girl with a cup of beer in my hand. Out of nowhere, the miraculous happened! Tyler, who had been socializing at another part of the house party, comes to me with great excitement and tells me that he just ran into a girl that went to the same high school as he did, and she was driving home to the Pittsburgh, Pennsylvania area the next morning! I smiled and looked at him in disbelief. I thought he was playing a joke on me. What are the odds of Tyler running into a high school friend from Pennsylvania, all the way in Ohio? What are the odds that this friend from Pennsylvania would choose to go to Ohio State University? What are the odds that this friend would choose to be in this small house in this party, out of all the parties on campus? Only The Lord Jesus could guide our steps to lead us directly to one another! Unbeknownst to us, we had been guided by the grace of The Lord, from the moment we entered the car to leave Indiana University Campus.

We marveled at the odds of this happening. We exchanged numbers, and agreed to meet first thing in the morning. We enjoyed ourselves at the party for a few more hours, and when we returned to the dorms, the Ohio State freshman wrestlers generously offered us extra bunk beds to sleep in. We woke up early the next morning, showered, and then had a nice breakfast. Tyler's friend from high school had arrived. We took many memorable pictures with our newfound wrestling companions. We exchanged contact information, hugged, and thanked them for their immeasurable hospitality. We entered the car and drove away.

That was the last time we saw those great men. But I am certain that The Lord will cause our paths to cross again.

We had an amazing time in the Pittsburgh area of Pennsylvania, where Tyler and his family lived. I got to meet his wonderful parents and his brother, who was just a few years younger. I immediately realized where Tyler got his great personality from. It was no wonder why Tyler and I had so much chemistry and were best of friends from the start.

During that week, Tyler drove me around to meet all his high school friends. We worked out and went to practice by ourselves each morning.

I can't forget the night that he took me to see his friend, the daughter of one of the wealthiest men in Pennsylvania. The mansion was gigantic! It was absolutely majestic! You could almost hear an echo in the house when you spoke. Up to this day, as I am writing, I can't say that I've been in a house that grand since then. And the family was very down to earth. It was truly an inspiration to be welcomed into such a grand and beautiful home.

We spent the remainder of the vacation getting into all sorts of mischief and hanging out with Tyler's old high school friends.

The night before we were to leave Pennsylvania to return back to campus, our teammate Caleb, who was from Philadelphia, Pennsylvania showed up out of the blue, with his yellow, pick-up truck. The three of us hung out all night, watching movies in Tyler's parents' living room until we fell asleep, and then drove back to Indiana the next morning.

What an amazing adventure that was! I remember, when we got back to the dorms, our floor's resident assistant gathered all the students on our second floor so that we could share any amazing stories about our Thanksgiving holiday experience. Most of the fifty or so guys were hesitant to share their stories.

After I heard less than a handful of everyday, typical Thanksgiving holiday stories told by my fellow floormates, I couldn't help but to share my unbelievable story with the group. After I had finished telling my story with such excitement and passion, the room stood amazed, and in awe of the unbelievable series of events that Tyler and I experienced.

After all the stories where told, to our surprise, our resident assistant told us that the reason that he asked us to share our stories, was to give a shopping gift certificate to the person with the most amazing story. As soon as he told us that, everyone in the room immediately smiled, knowing that I had definitely won, hands down.

I remember telling that story with such enthusiasm and detail, capturing my floormates' imaginations and taking them to the specific moments that I had just lived. It is certain that when you speak with love, unexpected goodness follows!

Chapter 4

Freshman year was steadily moving forward. My weeks consisted of a routine act of going to class, wrestling practice, and weekend celebrations with the many great friends that I was making.

Soon, it was time for the Christmas holiday season. Once again, I had no money to fly home to New Jersey, and as much as I missed my family, I wasn't the least bit upset about not going back to Irvington, New Jersey. I had been exposed to the truth in the world. I was living in a dream. There was no way that I was going back to the ghetto.

Almost all of my friends and teammates offered to have me come spend the Christmas holidays with their families. I decided this time, to spend it with one of my other freshman teammates and best friend, Gabriel.

The trip was not as unbelievable as the trip to Pennsylvania with Tyler, but it was definitely a wonderful experience. Soon, my best friend Gabriel and I were on a road trip to his parents' house in Naperville, Illinois, a small upper middle class town, just minutes outside of Chicago.

When we arrived at Gabriel's parents' home, I was just amazed by their beautiful big home, located on a quiet suburban cul-de-sac (I never knew what a cal-de-sac was before then). I was learning something new every day. The house had a shared pond, with sprawling green lawn in the back yard. I wanted to live there forever!

Gabriel's parents, who were from the country of Turkey, were simply amazing human beings. They were very kind and friendly to me and immediately treated me as part of the family. Gabriel had a cool, younger brother in high school and the cutest three or four year old little sister. Like all children, she put a smile on my face whenever she was around. Gabriel was truly blessed to have such a wonderful family and home.

More and more now, I was being inspired to strive to achieve success in the future. My eyes were being opened to the endless possibilities that The Lord had to offer me. Just like my other best friend Tyler had done in Pennsylvania, Gabriel showed me a great time in Illinois, introducing me to all his hometown friends at parties and in the neighborhood.

We trained daily, preparing ourselves for the upcoming wrestling season. We ate good food, and had a great holiday. For the first time in my life, I was spending the Christmas holidays away from my family. The experience was very new and refreshing to me. I was truly blessed to have such a friend in Gabriel.

Upon returning back to Indiana University campus for my last semester as a freshman, there was a name tag on my door letting me know that I had a new roommate. My other roommate, the six and a half foot tall, 400 plus pound kid had moved out about a month or two prior. My late night adventures were just too much for him to handle.

James Hill – my new roommate. What a guy! James was just the best guy out there. James was an Indiana University tennis player who had just transferred there from Czech Republic. His English was a little off, so I used to help him whenever it was necessary. It was great rooming with him. We made jokes and laughed all the time. I truly miss him. We used to encourage one another daily. He taught me a lot about tennis, and I taught him about wrestling. It puts a smile on my face, just thinking about the good times James and I had as roommates. James was definitely a genuine and pure person.

Times were great, but I had to think fast! Just as the first semester had flown by before my eyes, I knew that within a matter of months, summer would be here, and the school year would be over. There would be no more upfront financed payments by Indiana University toward my tuition and room and board.

By then, I had made so many lifetime friends and had become accustomed to living a good life in the most wonderful environment. There was absolutely no way in the world that I was going to leave my new life and return to living in the ghetto.

Another good friend who knew my financial dilemma and I were trying to figure out what to do before it was too late. My time was running out. I spent many nights pondering what to do.

Then one day, I heard some friends say in a joking manner, that an Indiana University student's tuition was paid for, as part of a court settlement, after being hit by a campus bus. They mentioned it jokingly, but a light immediately went off in my head. They had no idea how much in love with Indiana University I was, and how desperate I was to stay there. But was I going to run in front of a moving bus? I was desperate and in love, but I wasn't suicidal or that crazy.

A few days after contemplating what to do, I told my buddy that I was going to purposely slip and fall on the floor of our dormitory bathroom. I felt terrible. I knew that this was a very immoral (and illegal) act to do, but once I decided I was going to do it, there was no turning back. I remember that I kept telling myself that I would pay Indiana University back after I graduated and became a successful doctor or professional athlete. How naive I was, thinking that it was ok for one to do evil to achieve something good.

Never allow voices to convince you that it is ever ok to do evil to achieve something good! It is a crafty and common lie often used by the devil!

I tossed and turned all night, having second thoughts and thinking of all the possibilities that my plan could go wrong.

Finally, early the next morning, at about 6am, I awoke, sitting alone quietly on the edge of my bed. James had either slept over at another friend's room, or he must have already left for an early morning practice. I thought about it one last time, and then my mind was set. I was actually going to do it. I stood up, walked to my dorm room door and opened it. There wasn't a sound in the empty hallway. I slowly walked to the bathroom with a million thoughts running through my head. When I entered the bathroom, there was only one floormate in the shower. I ran some water from the sink and made a small puddle of water on the bathroom floor. I paused briefly, knowing that there would be no turning back from what I was about to do. I rehearsed in my head exactly how I was going to slip and fall, imagining my feet up in the air as my back and rear of my head broke my fall.

"Ahh...!"

I yelled at the top of my voice, making sure that whoever was in the shower heard me. I acted out the fall so well that I actually had a slight concussion when the back of my head hit the hard, wet, tiled bathroom floor. I laid there on my back groaning and moaning for what seemed to be an eternity, until the kid got out of the shower.

The most baffling and strangest thing that amazes me, even to this day, whenever I think about it, happened after the kid finished showering. The kid, who was a bit of a recluse, got out of the shower, saw me on my back in apparent pain and limited movement. And he, with an emotionless look on his face, stepped right over me, as if I weren't even there. He then opened the bathroom door, and walked out without saying a single word.

For a moment there, a part of me thought that maybe my concussion was worse than I imagined, or maybe I was dreaming. The kid was probably the quietest and reserved guy on our floor, but I couldn't believe that a person would walk right over another human being in pain. Perhaps, it was a sign from God that He was extremely disappointed in what I was doing. Or perhaps, the kid just didn't care. Perhaps, both... I may never know.

Moments later, other friends on the floor walked in the bathroom. And to their surprise, I was laying on the floor in apparent pain. They asked me what happened. And with a groan, I told them that I had slipped on the puddle of water and could not get up. Someone called an ambulance, and soon, within minutes, I was surrounded by paramedics and the majority of the boys on our second floor dormitory. The paramedics braced my neck, placed me on a stretcher, rolled me outside the dorms and into the ambulance. During the ambulance ride to the hospital, I recall one of the paramedics asking me if I were a believer in Jesus Christ.

I replied, "Yes... I am."

He then asked me if he could say a prayer for me. I agreed.

Despite all the sins I had committed in my life before that morning, as the paramedic prayed, that was the worst that my conscience had ever felt. But at that point, there was definitely no turning back. I could not just get up from the stretcher, remove my neck brace, and tell the paramedics to drop me off at the closest traffic light on the way to biology class. I would have been sent straight to jail.

I spent about two nights in Bloomington Hospital. I remember very little except how nice the nurses and doctors were to me and that they gave me lots of pain drugs orally and intravenously. I was only in slight pain from the small bump that I had caused on the back of my head. But whenever the nurses and doctors examined me to see whether I was in pain or not, I would keep telling them that my neck and back still hurt badly. Each time I told them that, I would be given more pain killers. Before I knew it, I was drowsy and euphoric than ever before!

I vaguely remember my teammates coming to visit me in the hospital. I was so touched. I honestly could not believe that they were there to see me. I had never been hurt and had to sleep in a hospital before. I was so surprised to know that I had friends who cared enough to take the time to come and visit me. Up to that day, I honestly thought that that only happened on television and in movies. It is so amazing to discover how many wonders and blessings there are in the world! I was learning a lot about people and the world. I was learning a lot about friendship and love. More and more, I began to realize what real friends were.

Days later, I was released from the hospital with a few prescription bottles of pain killers and sleep aids to return to the dorms. My friends told me that when they came to visit me, I was completely delirious. They said that I was extremely high on pain medications, and that I was slurring funny jokes and rambling about completely random topics. We all got a laugh about it.

Now that the first part of my plan was complete, I had to decide how I was going to pursue the second half of getting the school to cover my tuition. I was so naive. I had no idea how the legal process worked. I thought the school would immediately call my dorm room and offer to pay my tuition to avoid a major lawsuit from me.

A few days after not hearing anything from the school, I decided that I was going to call the school and ask them if they would be willing to give me an offer for my accident. I shake my head now, thinking of how foolish, young and ignorant I was. The man on the other end of the phone asked me who suggested that I call them. I told them that my friends and family suggested that I do so. He definitely must have known that I was desperate for money. He told me that they would investigate the matter and get back to me. For obvious reasons, I never heard back from him.

Next, I called all the top lawyers in the phonebook to represent me, however most of them already represented Indiana University, or charged a huge upfront premium before they would handle my case.

Finally, I found an attorney who agreed to charge a fee contingent on me winning the case. After asking me a number of questions, the lawyer agreed to meet with me in my dorm room. My plan was in motion.

When the lawyer arrived, he interviewed me, took some pictures of me with the neck brace around my neck, as well as the bathroom that had caution tape and "wet floor" signs where the accident happened. Before he left, he advised me to make sure that I went to all my doctor's appointments, and that he would be in touch. I couldn't believe it. My immoral plan was actually working.

Now, anyone pretending to be as injured as I was would have taken it easy and stayed in during the weekends. However, that anyone was certainly not me. By that time, I had become too much of a socialite to stay cooped up in my dorm room while all my friends were calling me to go out with them. I couldn't resist.

I remember getting drunk and going to all night parties with my neck brace wrapped around my neck. One night, with my neck brace on, I even did back tuck somersaults from ten foot high ledges to entertain my friends. I was probably being watched and recorded on video by insurance investigators. Some nights, I remember taking off my neck brace and going to parties. The neck brace was starting to get a bit embarrassing to have on at parties – even for me.

One night, I met the most beautiful bleach blond haired girl at a fraternity party without the neck brace on my neck. (By now you can tell that I had a thing for bleach blond haired white girls.) We danced and kissed passionately the entire night. At the end of the night, we exchanged numbers. The following evening, I called her, and she invited me to her dorm room. When I showed up at her door, less than 48 hours after meeting her, with a big neck brace wrapped around my neck, she was surely surprised. You should have seen the puzzled look that she had on her face.

Chapter 5

Then there was the night that I met Stella and Charlotte! I remember it like it was yesterday. It was the Martin Luther King Holiday, about a week after I met the beautiful bleach blond haired girl. I remember not returning the beautiful girl's calls, who wanted to get together that night. That's how I was. I was never satisfied with just one beautiful girl. I didn't want to be tied down, despite how gorgeous the girl was. I knew that there were just too many beautiful women on campus.

One of my floormates, Owen and I went to a fraternity party that night. And as usual, I was dancing on the stage, dancing with and making out with many different girls. And that's when Stella came out of nowhere. All of a sudden, I was dancing with this cute, blond, petite girl with her greenish, hazel eyes fixed into mine. I didn't know where she came from, but we were both there in the moment. As with the other girls that I danced with each time I went out, our lips were locked within minutes.

I don't know what it is, but I've always loved the feeling of kissing beautiful women, sometimes, even more than having sex. I feel a closer and more intimate and genuine connection with the woman while we are kissing. As if the woman is surrendering herself and her heart to me, and is sinking into a deep bliss of love.

Stella's friend Charlotte, was dancing with and kissing my friend Owen in the corner, on the wall just a few feet away. I thought we were just going to dance for a few songs, and then I would do my routine of telling her that I would be right back, and not see her for the rest of the night. Little did I know that Stella would have the most impact in my life for many years to come. We never departed sights. We danced and kissed the night away. Suddenly, the music came to an abrupt pause. The entire room panicked, with the knowledge of exactly what was going on. It was another campus police party shutdown. Indiana University is a dry campus, meaning that we weren't supposed to have alcohol. So the campus police routinely showed up at parties to shut them down. We all spent the next hour trapped in the huge fraternity house with hundreds of other students afraid to go outside as drunk as they were. I however, was never worried, but in retrospect, I realize how much more nervous Stella and Charlotte were.

Pausing for a moment, talking about the first time I met my former love, Stella, brought back so many fond memories of her. For the last week or two, I've been meaning to send her a funny message saying, "So umm...when are you gonna make me an uncle?" Then just minutes ago, I got on her Facebook page to send her the message, and to my complete surprise, I immediately noticed a handful of comments congratulating her since yesterday. How amazing! My dear friend is having a baby!

But for now, flashback to that evening.

"Which dorms do you guys live in?" I asked, as Stella and Charlotte gave us a ride back to our dorms in their old, maroon colored car.

"Oh...we live in McNutt." Stella quickly replied.

I realized a few days later, after talking to her on the phone, that they weren't really freshman. Stella was a senior in high school, and Charlotte was only a junior in high school. High schoolers at a college fraternity party...? I probably would have lied too. The girls dropped Owen and me in front of our dormitory building, Foster Harper. All of us were still slightly drunk. Stella and I kissed outside the car for a few more minutes and took some more pictures on my camera, which I kept for memories for years, up until losing them recently.

I spent the next couple of nights on the phone, sweet talking Stella, and the other blond haired girl that I had met just the week before meeting Stella. I was also sweet talking Alexis, the Vietnamese girl that I lost my virginity to, and a handful of other girls at the same time. It was a juggling act for me. I loved the excitement it gave me. Of course, I professed my undivided love to all of the girls, telling them everything they wanted to hear under the stars. It was all just a fun game to me.

Days after many phone conversations, I invited Stella over to my dorm. I knew that I was going to have sex, technically for the first time, since I never fully penetrated Alexis. This time, I was actually going to lose my virginity (for the second time).

It was a sunny afternoon. My roommate, James was away in class. My excitement grew as I did some last minute cleaning up while waiting for Stella to arrive.

Finally, she called and told me that she had arrived. When she came into my room, we spoke for some time, and then we started kissing. I laid her on my bed. I caressed her body and had passionate sex with her for about a half an hour. This time it was real.

I remember thinking to myself, "Finally, I'm not a virgin anymore…! Finally!"

When we finished having sex, Stella had a bashful, slightly embarrassed, and vulnerable look on her face. I gave her a kiss, got out of the bed, with sweat dripping all over my body, and left my room to go to the bathroom on our floor with a beach towel wrapped around my waste. I had the biggest smile on my face. I couldn't contain my excitement.

After I dried off in the bathroom and went into the hallway, all the guys on the floor at the time were giving me high fives.

"Who is she?" they asked with inquisitive smirks on their faces. "Give me all the details...!" some exclaimed.

I remember being in my next door neighbor's room, giving him every detail as he anxiously listened to every word.

"Oh, I know Stella…!" he exclaimed.

It turned out, after me giving Stella's description and name, that he even knew her from high school. When I returned to my room, Stella had made my bed, and was getting dressed with the same bashful look, rosy cheeks, and a slight smile on her face. I smiled back as our eyes connected. We both were thinking the same thing. After she was fully dressed, she kissed me goodbye, told me to call her, and left my room.

After she left, I jumped up in the air with excitement!

"I did it!"

It was a good day for me.

Later on, while I was changing my sheets, I noticed a few small blood stains on my sheets and pillowcase. I was a bit confused. Naively, I checked my body to see whether I had unknowingly cut myself by accident. My friends later told me that she was most likely a virgin before that afternoon. My already inflated pride grew larger. Two virgins, Alexis and Stella, in such a short time? It was wrong and immature, and I'm a completely different man now, but back then, it was like a badge of honor amongst the guys, to take a girl's virginity. It gave us bragging rights. Little did the guys on my floor, or Stella know that she had technically just taken my virginity.

I didn't tell Stella that when we had sex, I was still technically a virgin, until years later, during my fourth year in Indiana. I knew that telling her that I was a virgin would leave me extremely vulnerable. It would give her far too much power and leverage over me. All along, she was under the impression that I had had sex with countless girls in high school and my brief time during my freshman year in college, before meeting her. Over the years, from time to time, whenever she would get on my nerves, I would bring up the fact that I had taken her virginity to playfully tease her.

About a week later, Alexis, the Vietnamese high school senior girl that I had slept with first, drove miles in a rain storm to come and visit me. My floormates would soon see her going into my room. They thought I really was the man.

If the dictionary defines a womanizer as: A man who likes many women and has short sexual relationships with them; A habitual seducer of women; A man who philanders; A man who has casual sex frequently with a series of different women; A man with little concern for his conquest's feelings after intimacy has occurred, and is 'unable' to be sexually monogamous, or is matter-of-fact regarding his sexual exploits, then that was certainly me! I was definitely a womanizer! I was young and free. I did not want to be tied down or commit to any one girl. There were just an infinite amount of choices of beautiful women in Indiana University Campus. For the entire time that I was there, there literally wasn't one day that you couldn't be walking down the sidewalk and point in any direction, left, right, or behind you, (sometimes, even above you), without pointing at an amazingly beautiful girl. There were that many! And as a college athlete, different girls would flock to me on a daily basis. There was a lot of pressure and temptation, but I definitely wasn't complaining. I realized it, and took full advantage of it. I wanted to have sex and make out with as many beautiful girls as possible, just so that I could brag to my older brother on the phone, and to my friends and teammates on campus.

I had so many sexual encounters during my freshman year. I remember the time that I rode my bike downhill, completely drunk on alcohol, from my dorms to a girl's dorm late one night, at about 4am in the morning. I had just met her a few days before, and now she wanted to have sex with me. There I was peddling to her dorms, hardly able to keep balance on my bike, swaying from left to right. When I finally arrived to her dorm room, we had steamy, drunken sex for about an hour. Just a few minutes after we finished, and when she was getting ready to cuddle with me until morning time, I told her that I had to leave because I had early morning wrestling practice, which was true, except that practice wasn't that early in the morning. I could have stayed for a few more hours, but in my mind, that was probably the last time I was going to see her. Like a Roman soldier, I was off to my next conquest!

Then, there were the times when I went to parties and dance clubs and made out with about twenty different girls within the three or four hours that I was there with my friends. I'm not sure how it happened. I just know that there was a lot of alcohol involved, and I found myself always dancing with and staring in different girls eyes every few minutes.

Next, there was the time that Tyler, one of my best friends on the wrestling team, who I went to Pennsylvania with, during the Thanksgiving holiday, invited me to go with him to hang out with some beautiful, tall Indiana University ballerina girls. He had my attention. The second that he said the words 'ballerina girls', he needed say no more. There has always been something attracting to me, about the flexibility, agility, and gracefulness of ballerinas. I had never met a ballerina before, so I definitely agreed to go. I recall walking all the way across to the other end of campus with Tyler that evening. We arrived at the ballerina girls' dorm. We had been hanging out and talking for a few minutes. The next thing I know, within minutes of meeting the girls, I was on top of a girl, both of us naked, and locked in the floor's study lounge with the lights out. I believe we were both slightly intoxicated. Still quite sexually inexperienced, I remember naively thinking that we were having sex, as I rubbed up and down between her legs. I don't think I penetrated into her. I'm almost certain that she was a virgin too. I remember her face vividly to this day. She was a beautiful petit girl, with long, red hair, and had freckles on her face. She wasn't a ballerina, but I think she was a friend of theirs. After we got dressed, we exchanged phone numbers, and as usual, I promised to call her. Of course, I didn't. She ended up being in my biology class years later. She never said a word to me, but I can't blame her. I wouldn't have spoken to a philanderer like me either. Throughout all my great times and sexual expeditions in Indiana University, my time was quickly running out. Still looming was the lawsuit that I was filing against the school. Still looming was the fact that this may be my last year in my new found paradise. Still looming was the fact that I may have to return home to the ghetto. I had no job, and no income.

I remember even going to the record store one day, after much brainstorming, and buying all the top 20 music albums that I had googled. I also bought a bulk amount of blank CD's and took days burning the music onto the blank CD's with my neighbor's and teammate's computers, then going door to door, for many days, selling the counterfeit CD's to students. I told them the truth. I told them that I had run out of money for school and I was trying to raise money for my expenses. Sometimes, resident advisors and students would call security, and I would get chased out of the dorms. But that didn't deter me. I was on to the next dorm. I made so much money selling copied CD's to students, that I thought that I could do it forever. But then, after a while, the money stopped coming in.

Chapter 6

And then it began! One night, while my friends and I were drinking in my room, just before we went out, one of them asked me if he could get one of my pain medications that the doctor had prescribed for me after going to the hospital for the fall. I was a bit confused. I thought he was crazy. Before that night, I had never heard of anyone taking prescription medications as a recreational drug. I only had knowledge about common street drugs like marijuana. My eyes had never even seen cocaine until my first month in college. So, as far as prescription pills, this was completely new to me. "Yeah... I guess..." I responded.

It wasn't as if I had been taking the pain killers. All my life, I've always been against taking any type of prescription, or even common, over-the-counter medicines. I've always believed that my immune system was exceptionally strong enough for my body to self-heal. So, real injury or not, I wasn't interested in taking the pain and sleep medications that the doctor had prescribed for me.

"What does it do to you?" I curiously asked them.

"It gets you high..." they answered with a smile.

Minutes later, we went out to a party. We returned back to the dorms, late at night, completely drunk. My friends asked me for more pills.

"Sure..." I said again.

Still, I couldn't grasp what the big deal was about prescription pills. But I figured that I might as well give a few to them, since the pills would be going into the trash eventually.

The next weekend, my friends asked me for a few pills again. Once more, I freely gave them away. This time, while we were out partying, I noticed that my friends sweated quite a bit more than usual, and how their pupils were dilated.

Then a few days later, during the week, a friend came to my room asking me for over about a dozen of my prescription medications. As usual, I gave it to him. He left my room. Just minutes later, I heard a knock on my door. It was my buddy again, on the opposite side of the door. I opened the door and let him in. This time, he wasn't asking for more pills. He handed me almost $100 dollars in cash.

"What's this for?" I asked him puzzled but gracious.

He had sold the majority of the pills that I had given him to another student on the floor. If I thought my friends were crazy before, now I was sure that they were!

"You don't have to pay me. It's free..." I said, as I stretched my hands out to give him back the money.

My friend, not feeling right about profiting from selling my pills, insisted that I keep the money. I finally agreed. I figured that in my situation, I could use any extra money I could get. Plus, I thought that it was just a one time occurrence that someone would actually pay for prescription pills. I had much to learn...

When the weekend came around again, the word that I had prescription pills had spread rapidly through our dorm building. Another friend asked me if he could pay me for some pills. I agreed, and made about $50 dollars for about a dozen pills. And when he left my room, that's when a light went off in my head!

"I've got it!" I thought to myself with excitement. "This is how I'm going to pay for my college tuition!"

As always, whenever I stumble upon a new money making opportunity, my mind automatically turns into a super-calculator. I started doing the math in my head. I knew that I had more prescription refills left. Also, I knew that other students had different prescription medications that they could sell to me at wholesale prices, once my refills were finished. Then I would sell them to other students at marked-up prices.

I set my profit goal moderately. I figured that if I could make $100 dollars profit a day, then that would be $700 dollars per week in profits, $2,800 dollars per month, and $36,500 dollars profit per year. With my tuition balance of $24,000 dollars per year, $36,500 dollars would be more than enough to pay for school, and have extra money left over for other bills, entertainment and shopping expenses. It was a eureka moment for me!

The following weekend, just before my friends and I started drinking before going out, I decided to take one of my prescription medications to see what all the fuss was about. My back was slightly in pain that week from wrestling practice, so I convinced myself that I might as well take one.

I had a fun night out, however, I didn't feel much of a difference from what I usually felt when I just drank alcohol, and I was too strong willed to get addicted to the pills. The only thing on my mind was profit.

For the next few weeks, I was selling my pills, refilling my prescriptions, and buying in wholesale from fellow college mates. I was making hundreds of dollars every week. I was also carelessly spending a lot of the money that I made. I thought I was on top of the world. When the prescription pills finally ran out, there was only one other option for me to consider... Marijuana!

I thought long and hard, whether I wanted to get into that world. Selling prescription pills to my friends was wrong and illegal, however, getting involved in dealing marijuana, at such an early age of 18 years old, was a different story. If I was ever caught and accused of selling pain medications, I knew I could always say that my doctor prescribed them to me, and that the buyer found them in my room and took them without my knowledge or consent. In the worst case scenario, if they didn't believe me, I would just get a slap on the wrist by school officials, and be put on academic probation, or would have to do community service, which I was prepared to do.

However, if I was caught dealing marijuana, let alone in possession of marijuana, I would be facing much more severe charges, punishments, and possible expulsion from Indiana University, which would have defeated the cause of the original reason of selling drugs to pay for school.

After carelessly spending the majority of the money that I had earned in the previous weeks on clothes, bills, and friends, I had but a few hundred dollars left. Just like that, I was back to square one.

In the early spring of 2002, I gathered my last couple of hundred dollars, and bought my first ounce of marijuana. I was now in the big leagues! That day, I called and texted almost everyone in my phone book, telling them that I had marijuana. I wasn't ashamed or embarrassed that I was a drug dealer. It actually made me even more popular on campus than I already was.

At first, I spoke carelessly and freely about the drugs on the phone. I didn't believe that police officers actually taped phones. I thought they only did that in the movies. But then, I quickly learned after speaking to my paranoid and experienced customers, that I should be more discrete, and use code names and slang for the drugs, if I didn't want to scare away potential customers into thinking that I was an informant or cop. I also quickly learned to be much more discrete, if I wanted to avoid being caught and sent to jail. It took being hung up on once, by an experienced and paranoid customer, to fully understand the seriousness of the new business that I was in.

I remember how excited I was when I bought my first ounce of marijuana. Immediately, I sat in my dorm room calculating how much money I would make from that plastic bag full of marijuana.

For about a month, I didn't even know where to buy the small baggies that the marijuana was to be sold in. I remember wrapping the marijuana in aluminum foil. It was either aluminum foil or handing my customers the marijuana in their hands.

The aluminum foils quickly became my trade mark. Friends used to joke, telling me that they saw aluminum foil on the way to class, and that they immediately knew that it was from me. I also didn't have a scale to weigh the marijuana, as I divided it for sale. I had to borrow hand and digital scales from friends on my dorm floor.

Before that time, I had no idea that people paid for marijuana by the weight and quality of it. I remembered when I had found the small baggies of marijuana on the football field in high school. I thought I could just sell the marijuana, based on eyeing out the size of it. I had so much to learn. Compared to the marijuana that I had just bought, there was a huge difference in the quality, color, and scent. The marijuana that I had found back in high school was completely dry, flakey, brownish in color, and gave off a displeasing smell. On the other hand, the marijuana that I had just bought was moist, plump, sticky to the touch, had red hairs, white THC crystals, light green in color, and had a strong, fruity aroma. I had no idea that anything like that ever existed until that afternoon.

I remember losing money the first few days, thinking that the cost of marijuana of the high quality was the same as the cost of marijuana of low quality of the same size, from back in my hometown of Irvington, New Jersey. My friends eventually explained the difference to me. It was definitely a lesson learned.

It didn't matter though. I was going to make much bigger profits by selling 1 gram bags at a time, rather than the common 3.5 gram bags, called eighths (as in 1/8 of an ounce). The fact that students were willing to pay up to $80 dollars at a time for eighths baffled me in itself. I couldn't believe it.

I asked myself after the first student bought an eighth, spending about $80 dollars, "How in the world can they afford it!? Why would people spend that much money on drugs!?"

The answer was beyond me. But I was not complaining. In the poor town of Irvington, New Jersey where I was from, people would find it hard to even spend as little as $5 dollars for lower quality marijuana. But here in college, $40 dollars to $80 dollars for an eighth was the norm. Most of my customers had never even heard of buying small $5 dollar and $10 dollar baggies of marijuana, called nickel and dime bags, until they started buying from me.

I knew that I was on to something! I decided that I was going to be one of the first drug dealers on campus to sell my marijuana in nickel and dime bags, in order to maximize my profits. Some students loved my idea, because it allowed them to buy from me without having to drive to the bank or ATM to get the extra money. Also, they didn't have to combine their money with other friends in order to afford to smoke.

Other students, of course, hated the idea, simply because when you did the math, you were paying slightly more money, per gram of marijuana. It didn't matter to me though. I knew that the supply was low, and that the demand was very high. I was accomplishing exactly what I had set out to do by selling smaller portions of marijuana at a time. I was maximizing my profits and making almost double the money per ounce that I was supposed to be making.

Chapter 7

Time was quickly passing by. My freshman year was winding down. After a few months of my injury lawyer investigating my case and communicating with me via telephone and mail, I received a final letter from my lawyer stating that he would not be able to work on my case anymore. I remember calling him and asking him the reason he would not continue to work on my case. He gave me a vague answer, something along the line of him feeling that he could not win the case. He suggested that I hire a lawyer that I had to pay for in advance. That was the last time I heard from him.

I can't say that I was upset at all. I felt as if a huge burden had been lifted from my shoulders. I decided not to pursue another attorney. My conscience was now clear to some degree. Besides, now I had another plan, in selling drugs to pay my tuition.

Then, there was the Indiana University major drug raid of 2002! There was much stir on campus when the news broke out. The police had busted dozens of students and faculty members allegedly involved in a drug dealing network. It was all over the news and the papers. The police raided the room of my neighbor just a few doors away from my room. I was very fortunate that I had only just started selling drugs.

The raid certainly made me be more careful and take greater precautions not to get caught. I understood that the more that I knew, the less likely chance I would have of being caught. I remember spending countless hours of my free time researching everything that I could learn about drug dealing and drugs, on the internet. I can't tell you how many times I watched the movies 'Blow' and 'Scarface' in my friend's dorm room. I watched those movies all the time. Like everything that I did, I wanted to be the most knowledgeable in the field. I wanted to be the best drug dealer on campus. I had the same energy and ambition as I had in high school, when I was selling boxes of chocolates and novelties door to door. To me, this was the same concept, except, instead of selling boxes of chocolates and novelties, I was selling illegal drugs.

By the last month of my freshman year in college, I was selling a laundry list of drugs to students, including marijuana, Xanax, Percocets, Darvocets, Klonopins, Oxycontin and other prescription drugs! My parents and the rest of my family back home had absolutely no idea what I was doing. I was doing all this, while still going to wrestling practice and classes. I remember staying up all night, writing multiple page papers, and getting calls from students wanting to meet up and buy marijuana and Adderall, well after midnight.

I remember when I tried Adderall for the first time, before writing a long sociology report. Adderall is a prescription drug for people with ADD (attention deficit disorder). It is supposed to make you concentrate and stay focused. Many students however, bought and used it, even though they weren't diagnosed with ADD. That night, against my reservations from putting any prescription, or even over-the-counter drugs in my body, I took a pill. I had never been able to stay that focused while typing a term paper like that before! It was an amazing feeling that I experienced! Unlike when I took the pain medication with alcohol before going to a party, I could understand why students were paying me money for this prescription drug. It felt like a super-drug! I felt like my brain had become advanced. It made me think that people taking this pill on a regular basis had a clear advantage over other people.

Before taking the Adderall, I couldn't even type at a normal speed, but after about two or three hours after taking the pill, I was using the computer keyboard as if I had been typing for years.

I remember taking the Adderall at about 9pm in the evening. Hours later, at about 6am the next morning, when I was done writing the paper, and tried to get at least an hour or two of sleep before going to my sociology class, my heart was still beating as fast as what seemed to be a million beats per second. Sleeping was futile. I feel blessed that I don't have an addictive personality, otherwise, I would have started taking that drug on a regular basis.

After a while, I started carrying the drugs in my pocket while typing papers in the computer lab. Some nights, I would start typing a paper in the computer lab with zero dollars in my pocket, and by the time I was done around five in the morning, when the sun was coming out and the birds were starting to chirp, I would have a few hundred dollars in my pocket, and completely sold out of the drugs that I had brought in my pocket.

I loved the feeling of being the most reliable drug dealer on campus. Day or night, while other drug dealers had turned off their cell phones and were asleep, I was always available and willing to sell. I was definitely one of the most popular kids in school... the big man on campus. I was an Indiana University wrestler and a drug dealer. I was the life of every party.

But just like that, my amazing freshman year had come to a close. I ended the school year failing my biology pre-med class, that I hadn't bought a book for during the year. I easily could have bought a biology book during the end of the year, when I started making money selling drugs, but by that point, it was far too late in the year to improve my failing grade. I did well in my other classes that I had books for.

It was now time to move on, and journey into an uncertain future. The school year had ended. I could not fathom going back to the ghetto after being in paradise for a year. It was pretty strange to me. A lot of friends invited me to their parents' home to spend the summer vacation with them. Once again, this type of hospitality and friendship was very new and foreign to me. I doubt that would have happened, where I was from.

I felt honored and gracious that my friends trusted and appreciated my friendship enough to invite me to their homes. However, I graciously turned down their offers, even though I had absolutely no solid plan about how I was going to survive on campus with the majority of the students and my friends away.

That was just another instance of me going with the flow. My mind was set that I was going to survive the summer in Bloomington! I called all around, looking for anyone who was staying on campus for the summer. Finally, one of the girls that I had been buying my marijuana from, said that I could probably stay at her place. But then, at the last minute, she said that there wasn't enough room for me. I wasn't sure if that was the truth or not, but it probably wouldn't have worked out living with and selling drugs out of one of my supplier's apartment.

I called one of my best buds and teammate Luke, who was going to be on campus attending summer school. He was a year or two ahead of me. I looked up to him. There wasn't much room in the apartment that he, another wrestler, and an IU baseball player lived in, but he said that it was ok for me to stay for the summer. I was very relieved.

I called Stella, last minute, and asked her whether she could come and give me a ride to the guys' house a few miles away.

"Ok." she said, without a second thought.

I couldn't believe it. I was shocked. I was expecting her to say no, or that she was too busy to take hours out of her day, driving from one end of town to another, to help me move.

Once again, I was amazed by the love that I was receiving. That honestly, may have been the first time that I truly knew, and fully understood what friends were. I was truly touched.

Alone in my dorm room, during the last day to check out of Foster Harper dormitory, with the campus virtually empty, as the majority of the students had packed up and traveled back home the day before, I sat there on my twin bunk bed, reminiscing about all the unforgettable fun times I got to experience during my freshmen year – from the first night that I arrived on campus and slept over at that Asian girl's condominium, to the time I awkwardly peddled my bike with one hand on the handlebar grips, and the other hand holding my heavy suitcase the next morning on my way to Eigenmenn dorms. To the time that my friend barged in while I was naked in bed, giving the Polish girl a massage – to the time I lost my virginity, and all my wild sexual encounters. And the time I finally turned 18, and was dancing at night, with music blasting, belligerently drunk, on top of my teammate's yellow pickup truck in front of Foster Harper dorms.

I reminisced about my and Tyler's crazy trip to Ohio State campus, on the way to his home in Pennsylvania – and the time my friends surprised me with a visit, while I was heavily medicated in the hospital. I recalled the crazy time that my friends and I got completely drunk one night and decided to drive over 60 miles, to the small town of Vincennes, with two or three of us freezing in the back of a pickup truck, as the driver speed down the dark open road. I remember being far too intoxicated to know where in the world I was. I just remember being in a cabin-like, secluded house, watching highlights of the New York Yankee baseball team just winning the World Series.

Alone in my dorm room, I remembered all the early morning wrestling practices where we freshman were completely hung over from drinking and partying just a few hours before. It's amazing. We all seemed to work even harder during those practices. Our coaches could smell the scent of alcohol coming from our breath and seeping through our pores as we began to sweat. I reminisced about the times that we ran up steep dirt hills in the woods carrying our teammates on our backs – to the times we ran up and down mountainous, dry, ski slopes – and all the countless fights with other students, we freshmen wrestlers were involved in, whenever we went out to parties together. I remember always being caught in the middle of a fight that a teammate had initiated. I never hit anyone. But I was always there holding people back.

There was one time, that we were at a house party, and a wrestler beat a kid up in a fraternity so badly. That's what usually happened when you mixed wrestlers with alcohol.

Just a week later, I ended up at that same student's fraternity's house party. I remember thinking to myself before I went in, that I had nothing to worry about, since I didn't throw any punches. About a half an hour after being in the huge, crowded fraternity house, the word started to spread that I was a wrestler.

Suddenly, I found myself surrounded by angry, drunk fraternity brothers that were planning on attacking me. I recall staying calm, and letting them know that I never threw a punch at their fraternity brother, and was sympathetic to what happened to him. I believe a few of them who were there confirmed that I was telling the truth, but they still wanted me out immediately.

I thank The Lord for delivering me out of danger at that moment. Now that I think back, as bad as my teammate damaged the fraternity brother's face, it could have been horrific, what a house full of angry, intoxicated fraternity brothers could have done to me. I could have been killed! Faithfully, I made it out unharmed.

When it came to fraternities though, I can honestly say that virtually all the fraternities on campus loved me, especially Sigma Pi and Sigma Nu. The feeling was mutual. I was practically an honorary brother at all the fraternities. There are just an infinite number of fond memories with them. One night, my friends and I walked home from a fraternity party, completely intoxicated as usual. We stood outside the back of the Foster Harper's nine story dormitory at about 4am in the morning, repeatingly singing "Na na na nah, na na na nah, hey hey eh, good bye..." That had to have been one of the most fun nights I had during my freshman year. Students were yelling out of their windows, telling us to shut up. Some students were throwing food and water at us. Other students sang along with us from their windows. It's those innocent and simple moments in life that I cherish the most – more than any amount of money, or material objects, but moments like those.

Sitting there alone in my room on the last day of the school year, I also thought about how fortunate I was to have had such a great roommate in James. We had so many good times and laughs as roommates. I used to bring girls in the room late at night after returning from a party, and have sex with the girl in the bottom bunk. I remember always telling James to pretend to be sleeping. He would agree with a smile. When the girl would leave, we would joke and laugh for hours. I can only imagine the stories he has told his friends and family back home, in Czech Republic. They must think I'm a crazy man. I'll always remember the night that I returned to the dorms really drunk (drunker than usual), and he took care of me, making sure no one took advantage of me, or stole my possessions or baggies of marijuana in my room. It was funny hearing him say that I was so intoxicated, that I was speaking a different language to him.

Next, I thought about the night that one of my best friends and I walked to hang out at some good girl friends of ours' apartment. For the second time in my life, even after mentally vowing never to smoke marijuana again, I got high! Everyone in the apartment was smoking. I remember them teasing me and begging me to smoke with them. So, against my better judgment, I decided, "Why not...?", and joined in.

Before joining in, I told them the entire story of how I thought that I had died after smoking for the first time in high school and how I wound up struggling with my friend to lie down on the side walk in Queens, New York, late one evening.

I remember reasoning with myself, that maybe that was just a one-time negative experience. I had never smoked out of a bong before. They cheered me on. Like a clueless novice, instead of puckering my lips and inhaling from inside the mouth of the bong, I wrapped my big lips around the entire mouth of the big bong, as if I was going to eat it. Everyone got a good laugh out of it.

Then boom...! Just a few minutes after smoking and bragging, once again, that I didn't feel any effects, I was back in that parallel dimension again!

I thought I was dead again! I thought that life itself and the world was not real – just one big movie that I was unaware that I was in.

Perhaps, it is...

It did make me realize however, that everything was always going to end up ok – that there would be a magnificent and glorious ending for my life!

My universe had been altered within a blink of an eye. My heart began to beat faster. I began to panic, but I didn't want to make it obvious and embarrass myself as I did the last time I smoked as a high-schooler.

That night, everyone just laughed and laughed and laughed at me. I calmed my nerves by telling myself that in a few hours, when the THC from the marijuana wears out in my body, this uneasy feeling would all be over. Apparently, I was wrong. Hours later, the effect had intensified. It seemed that everyone just wouldn't stop laughing at me. I could only imagine the paranoid look on my face. I decided to sleep in order to escape the paranoid, uneasy feeling. I recall waking up the next day still feeling some of the after effects.

It took me a couple of days to feel 100% like myself again. For some reason, my mind and body reacts completely differently than most people after smoking marijuana.

Finally, I sat back alone in my dorm room on that last day of school reminiscing about the funny experience that I had when my teammate, Tyler (another teammate named Tyler) and I got stuck in the dormitory elevator. For days prior, I discovered that when you slightly opened the elevator doors while it was moving, the elevator would stop for a few seconds, and you could climb out onto whatever floor the elevator was closest to. To me, that was exciting.

I remember telling Tyler one day, how fun it was to do. Needless to say, he was not as enthused as I was. I opened the elevator door as it was in motion once, and then the elevator paused. Tyler became uneasy and a bit irritated. I opened the door twice, and then the elevator paused again. More irritated, Tyler was not laughing, and asked me to stop. I was entertaining myself, making him nervous, far too much to stop.

Finally, I opened the elevator door once more. This time, the door did not open more than a few inches, and we were stuck between the second and third floor. The panicked and upset look on Tyler's face was priceless. We were trapped in the elevator! After we realized that the elevator would not restart again, we yelled and rang the alarm for help. We spent over an hour in that small elevator.

Excited and amused, fellow dormmates slipped us pizza, drinks, and snacks through the small elevator opening after unsuccessfully trying to pry the elevator door open. It was a team mission.

Finally, firemen were able to get us out. I could tell that Tyler was pretty irritated about being trapped in the elevator, but we later laughed so hard about it. We became known as the elevator guys for the next couple of weeks. Another priceless moment for me...

There was never a dull moment, hanging out with my teammate Tyler and also, another teammate, Elijah. I smile as I think of the many nights that Elijah, Tyler, and I drove to parties, during weeknights, blasting old school rap and hip hop songs – and the time Tyler and Elijah drove me miles away from campus to climb high rock quarries. When we finally reached the peak of the rock quarries, the view was priceless! What a life! I had never done or experienced anything like that before!

I remember seeing Elijah, during my last year in Indiana University, strangely running through the streets, late at night, after a club. He weighed about 200 pounds of all muscle and had his hands pumping in the air, with no shirt, like the hulk, completely drunk. I had to do a double-take, as I watched him run by.

The time had now come for me to empty and exit my room and turn in my dorm keys. I was the only student left in the dormitory. Stella wasn't due to arrive until another hour or so. I turned in my keys and packed all of my possessions downstairs to the front of the dormitory building and quietly waited.

There I was alone, sitting on a gray, foldable beer chair, under the hot sun, surrounded by all my possessions on the pavement when Stella's old maroon sedan came rolling into the driveway in front of Foster Harper. We both smiled at the irony of the situation. We both knew exactly what one another was thinking at that moment. "Where did I find this person?"

Chapter 8

I didn't bring any drugs to my new roommates' apartment. I slept on the futon in the living room and spent most of my initial days there contemplating my next move.

My teammates did not want me to get lazy and complacent in the apartment while they were away in classes during the day, so they pressured me into getting a job.

So a few weeks into my summer break, I got my fourth job, next to my brief times at Dunkin Donuts, Successful Teens door-to-door sales, and the brief construction work after high school. I was hired as a telemarketer, selling DVD's, at a company called Dial America, just three blocks away from the apartment. For me, it was easy money. All I had to do was wait for the person to pick up the phone, and then convince them to order a subscription of popular DVD's.

Soon, I was making hundreds of dollars a week. Daily, I was top salesperson. Because I had so much experience selling door-to-door while a high school student, I more than excelled in telemarketing. I made it as fun as I could.

But at the end of the day, it just wasn't for me. This job would not pay for my bills and cover my tuition. I had much grander plans in mind – drug dealing!

A few weeks into my summer, I was walking through the mall, with my usual tank top, shorts, and sandals, when a beautiful girl with long flowing hair stopped me, and asked if I was a soccer player.

"No... I wrestle." I replied, completely caught by surprise.

This was the first time that a girl had approached me in the mall. We introduced ourselves. She told me that her name was Natalie. We talked for a short while, and then exchanged numbers.

The following night, she and some friends stopped by the apartment to hang out. It turned out that she had just graduated high school and knew Stella and the crew of Bloomington locals. I liked her a lot. We had an undeniable chemistry right from the start. We started dating.

With all the previous girls that I had been with during my freshman year, she was really my first actual girlfriend. I didn't cheat on her, nor did I remain a womanizing player while we were together. For the first time in my life, I knew what it felt like to have a real girlfriend that I was in love with. We had so much fun together. I remember the countless afternoons and nights that she came over and spent time in the pool with me. I remember the long walks we had through campus, and the many kisses we shared when we were together. And the sex – the sex was amazing! I really loved her. What a girl she was! She really made me happy. Stella was still in the picture though. However, Stella knew that my attention was elsewhere.

By midsummer, my teammates that I was living with, were done with their summer school classes. They packed up some of their possessions and went home for the summer, leaving me alone in the apartment. A few days later, my urge to deal drugs had returned. I immediately quit my job, and I used my last checks from Dial America to buy a few ounces of marijuana. I was back in business!

I called and texted everyone in my phonebook that was still in town, letting them know that I had marijuana. Within hours, I was making profits again.

For weeks, I was going out to parties and getting more and more customers. I would talk to anyone I met on the street, in the mall, and even pizza delivery boys. Almost everyone that I crossed path with knew that I was a drug dealer. I was a relentless and fearless marketer. My social skills were being mastered. I could talk to anyone, whether they be young or old, hateful or kind. I did not discriminate. I wanted to do business with everyone.

Then, one day, a new client of mine wanted to trade some of my marijuana for some of his ecstasy pills! It caught me by surprise. I didn't think there was a market for ecstasy. I couldn't think of much people that I would be able to sell them to. I gave it some serious thought.

First, I had already graduated from selling petty prescription pills to selling marijuana, which was bad in itself. Now, I was considering journeying down this dangerous, yet lucrative path.

What helped me make my decision was the fact that I would be making an incredibly more amount of money in an accelerated amount of time. I did the calculations in my head of how much more profit I would make if I continued selling 50, 100, 1000, and more pills within a year. Suddenly, paying for four years of tuition seemed very attainable. By that point, I was deep in the drug game, and I thought there was no turning back.

I traded my marijuana for a little under a few dozen ecstasy pills. Up until that point, I had never seen ecstasy in person. It was just a drug that I had always heard about. I remember it like it were yesterday, examining the ecstasy pills, as I held them in my hands. Beige omegas... They were small beige pills, stamped with the Greek omega symbol.

The second I left my supplier's sight, I sent a mass text message that I had ecstasy.

"I want them all!" many clients replied.

Within minutes, just like that, all the pills were sold! I had never seen anything like that before! A light bulb immediately went off in my head.

For the following days, I kept getting calls and text messages asking me if I could get more ecstasy pills. I called the kid that I had traded my marijuana for the ecstasy pills. This time, I asked for a few hundred pills! Since this was going to be a sudden, big transaction, the level of paranoia was heightened on both ends. Neither one of us was sure whether the other was an undercover police officer or an informant. I remember that my greatest argument, whenever someone thought that I was an undercover police officer, was: "I'm an IU wrestler! How can I be a cop?" That always seemed to put the other party at ease.

Despite, the kid that I was buying the few hundred pills of ecstasy from and I were extremely cautious toward one another. Against my better judgment, I agreed to leave almost one thousand dollars in a plastic bag, right outside the front door of the apartment. And he was supposed to take the money and leave the few hundred pills by the door. We did this so that just in case one of us was an informant or undercover police officer, there would not be any proof of hand to hand exchange of the drugs and money.

After I placed the money outside the apartment door, I waited impatiently for the kid to arrive at the door and exchange the drugs for the money. I was taking a huge risk! There was a chance that he could have taken the money and fled.

Finally, through the apartment window, I saw him quickly come to the apartment door and leave. Immediately after he left, I rushed and opened the door, looked down, and to my relief, I saw a black bag filled with pills. My excitement rose, as I counted the pills out on the table that night.

My girlfriend, Natalie was there the whole time and she still loved me. Sometimes, I thought of her as George Jung's first girlfriend, in the movie 'Blow', who he was madly in love with throughout his drug dealing days. We really loved and cared for each other, no matter what.

This time, the kid had sold me different pills. They were white in color, and about double the size of the previous 'omega' pills. Plus, they were engraved with a logo of what looked like an arrow.

"What are they called?" I asked him on the phone that night.

"They're Christmas trees or arrows." he replied.

Once again, I sent out a mass text message, that I had just gotten more ecstasy. Within a few days, all the pills were sold!

Then, the complaints started coming in. Some of my customers had no problem, however, the majority of customers said that they didn't feel any effect. I was shocked and surprised. I didn't do ecstasy, so there was no way I could know for myself.

I decided to go on the internet to research ecstasy pills with the 'Christmas tree' and 'arrow' logo. After minutes of searching, there they were, right on my computer screen. Caffeine pills! The guy had sold me a few hundred caffeine pills!

I was furious. I could not believe that I had been hustled. I immediately called my supplier, demanding a refund. He told me that he got those pills, last minute, from a different supplier than he had gotten the 'omega' ecstasy pills from, and he had no idea that they were fake pills. I called him for months after, but needless to say, I never saw him again.

I was a bit puzzled though, some customers who had tried it insisted that they were genuine ecstasy pills and wanted more. Maybe, they mistook the caffeine rush for an ecstasy roll. Or, it could have been psychological. What's remarkable about taking ecstasy is that they don't have to give the inducer an actual physical effect. Just as long as the inducer thinks he or she is ingesting genuine ecstasy, they will feel the effects.

Since I had read online, that the pills were only caffeine pills, and not ecstasy, but some customers insisted that they felt the effects, I decided to take two of the pills with some friends one night out and find out for myself. Still 18 years old, this was going to be my first time taking ecstasy (or not). What a surreal and fun night for me!

In retrospect, they were definitely caffeine pills, but the fact that there was a possibility that they were real ecstasy pills, made me think that I was rolling on ecstasy. And I guess that was the purpose of buying them.

I remember going to some girls' apartment with Stella and another friend around 4am in the morning, after a long night out. With the pills and alcohol still in my system, I smoked marijuana again and temporarily fell into the deepest, supernatural love with one of the girls, than I had ever been, up to this day! I can't count how many times that I told that girl that I loved her. It must have been the combination of the caffeine pills, the alcohol, and the marijuana in my system, coupled with the fact that I thought that I had ingested genuine ecstasy. You could only imagine the extreme euphoria that I was feeling!

A little over an hour later, around 5am in the morning, I remember driving back to the apartment with Stella. It was one of the most out of this world, psychedelic experiences that I have ever had! Even as I write these words now, many years later, I am taken back to that experience.

As Stella and I drove home, on the virtually empty campus streets, the whole world suddenly seemed absolutely perfect! I had never felt in love and at peace with the universe like I did that early summer morning. The trees were beautiful. They seemed to dance in unity amongst the breeze. The sky was lovely. The squirrels running across the grass were cuter than ever before. The vivid sounds were mystical. All my senses were magnified. There wasn't a care in the world. It was as if I was driving inside of a video game. Our mouths, totally dehydrated and cotton-mouthed, and hardly able to properly enunciate words, Stella and I laughed so hard during the entire, swerving, ride home. It's a wonder that we weren't pulled over by a police officer.

When we arrived at the apartment complex, instead of parking, I remember driving clear over the 6" inch parking lot ledge, and landing in the sandbox of the apartment complex's playground area. With the music in the car blaring loudly, I maneuvered as if I were driving a go-cart around and about the playground, laughing with Stella at the top of our lungs, until finally parking in a parking space. What a night...! What a morning!

Days later, it was time for me to go home to visit my family. After a year of being away from my parents, my brother and my sister, who I had missed so much, I finally flew back to Irvington, New Jersey. They all missed me so much and were excited to finally see my face again. When my brother and I got some time alone, I told him that I was selling drugs, going into detail about how exciting it was. I knew I could tell him anything. He was a bit concerned, but at that age, just a year and a half older than me, I think he was more excited than anything else.

After reuniting with my family, and spending about two great weeks with them, I was back on the plane to Bloomington, Indiana – back to my friends, back to my girlfriend Natalie, back to paradise! Business was calling, and I was there to answer!

Even in the early stages of my drug dealing days, I knew that I had to diversify my forms of income. Also, I was always looking for an alternative to drug dealing – a way to get out. One of the other roommates was an IU baseball player. He spent most of the time at his girlfriend's apartment at another part of the town, so he was hardly ever there until the last few weeks of summer, when it was time to move out.

He was the one who first taught me about stocks. I recall asking him every question that I could think about, every time I saw him come into the apartment to move his possessions. I immediately started paying attention to financial news on television and newspapers. I spent hour after hour researching information about stocks on the internet. A new vision of endless possibilities had suddenly appeared to me.

Then, after weeks of continuous research and endless questions, at the age of 18 years old, I bought my first stock – Google, Inc., for about $450 dollars.

With the summer winding down to an end, jealousy and lack of trust came into the picture, between my girlfriend, Natalie and me. Perhaps, we weren't meant to be more than an incredible summer romance. I remember one day, yelling at her on the phone, suddenly accusing her of being unfaithful to me, then immediately hanging up the phone on her.

Stella was at the apartment with me at the time, of course, cheering me on. Stella and I always joked about how she could always manage to get a girl that I was involved with, out of the picture. The truth is that I loved Natalie, but I just used the fact that she was possibly being unfaithful to me, as an excuse to break up with her. A new school year was about to begin. I wanted to be free, so I took advantage of the opportunity. The single, seductive and womanizing Maubrey was back!

Chapter 9

JUDGES

Before I knew it, a wonderful summer had quickly flown by. What was supposed to be my sophomore year in college had arrived. I desperately tried to register for classes, even though I had not paid the balance on the tuition bill from my freshman year. My attempts were futile. I moved out of my teammates' apartment just before the school year started.

At first, I had no idea where I wanted to live. I didn't plan that far ahead. But then, I decided that I wanted to live in the same apartment complex as my best friend and teammate, Gabriel.

The management of the apartment complex matched me with another Indiana University sophomore. His name was Dylan. I signed a one year lease in a shared two bedroom, two bathroom apartment, at the beautiful University Commons Apartments. The University Commons Apartments was one of the nicest apartment complexes around campus. I was so in love with the place. The apartment complex wasn't extravagant, or overly luxurious, but it was so pleasant and charming. Up until that point, I had never lived in such a wonderful complex.

The complex sat on top of a slightly sloped hill. When you slowly drove onto the grounds, you could see a basketball court, a sand volleyball court, picnic areas, and other amenities such as a resort-style swimming pool. We had a fitness center, a club house with a billiards table, table tennis, foosball tables, popcorn and vending machines, and flat screen televisions mounted on the walls.

When you entered our two bedroom fully furnished apartment, you could smell the aroma of our freshly vacuumed and steamed, gray carpeted apartment. You saw a fairly moderate sized living room, and a modest, yet, state-of-the-art kitchen, with an island bar table attached. You saw two private bedrooms, one to the left and the other to the right of the living room, each room equipped with private bathrooms. There was even a full-sized washer and dryer near the kitchen.

Finally, there was the private patio of our first floor apartment, over-looking the sprawling, manicured green grass that kissed the sparkling, man-made pond.

One of my favorite things to do was to relax on the patio, while watching the wonderful geese graze on the grass, and peacefully swimming in the pond.

My new environment was truly delightful. My new roommate, Dylan and I got along great. I remember meeting his parents during the move-in day. His dad was an attorney, so I instantly thought that if I were ever caught selling drugs, then I would have a friend's dad as a lawyer. Dylan was a good guy. He knew how to cook and bake really well. He taught me how to cook simple cuisines like grilled chicken and fettuccine. With his skills to cook, he definitely had my approval. Being that I was born in Germany, we bonded even more when I learned that he was fluent in the German language. I didn't understand the language, but I used to call my parents in New Jersey, from parties, around 2am in the morning, and let him speak German with my mom and dad.

As the initial days went by, I quickly found out that Dylan was adamant about neatness – even more than I was.

I can't forget the carpet incident. Dylan was upset that we didn't get brand new carpet as most of our friends in the apartment complex did. He called the management office to complain that there were a few stains on the carpet. But before the maintenance man came to take a look, we decided to get some ketchup and mustard and completely stain an entire square-foot section of the carpet with the condiments. It was a terrible thing to do, but we hadn't laughed that hard in a long, long time. I remember music playing loudly as we took turns dancing bare feet on the ketchup and mustard stains and taking pictures of our crime. It was the most amusing sight to see. I'm sure the management thought otherwise. Our plan worked though. A few days later, we had brand new carpet. How terrible we were.

And then there was Landon. I met Landon, one of Gabriel's roommates, again, after meeting him and going out to a few parties together during our freshmen year. I heard that he sold marijuana too, so we instantly partnered up. I told him that I was looking for a new ecstasy supplier. He said that he knew just the person. I was always looking for a cheaper supplier, so he introduced me to Carter.

When I met Carter in his apartment with Landon for the first time, I immediately knew that he was a big time dealer. Carter was the definition of a drug dealer. He had the big screen television, multiple video game consoles, the expensive car, nice furniture, fur rugs, diamond jewelry, expensive clothes, a nice apartment, and the girls. This was exactly what I wanted and dreamed about – and he had it all!

I was a lot more ambitious and a risk taker than Landon was. Landon stuck with only selling marijuana. However, I already had the clientele for marijuana and ecstasy. I started the year off with a bang! Everyone knew me. I spoke to, and networked with everyone that I could at all the house parties and night clubs that I went to. I would go to parties with many small baggies of marijuana and ecstasy pills and leave with hundreds of dollars in my pocket. I had no fear of dying or going to jail. My cell phone was ringing off the hook every day, and my contact list was getting larger every week. I was making so many new friends and contacts.

Soon, I bought my first big screen television. Next, my mind was set on buying a brand new, yellow Hummer, one of the latest and expensive cars at the time. I started saving all my money and reinvesting in buying bigger and bigger quantities of drugs, digital scales, and air and scent concealing machines.

My clients always used to offer to smoke marijuana or take ecstasy with me, but I always declined, reminding them that I was a student athlete, and wasn't into drugs. They used to be amazed at how I had the will power to have all those drugs and not smoke or ingest them. I was the ideal drug dealer. I was only interested in making profit, and nothing else.

The money was good, but it was never enough to live bountifully and pay for school at the same time. I knew that I had to take more risks and do bigger deals.

Week after week, I was selling out of drugs and using the majority of my profits to reinvest in buying bigger and bigger quantities of marijuana and ecstasy. It was a fast and exciting time for me. Every day, I would race to my cell phone when it rang. I had set my cell phone ringer to a special ambulance-like siren for all my clients. So I knew whenever money was calling. I was going to parties three to four nights a week. As my money and popularity increased, so did the beautiful women.

By then, I decided that I wanted to be the biggest drug dealer in the country! I wanted to be an expert. I got online almost daily, and read everything that I could about all the major street drugs and even the uncommon drugs. I promised myself that I never would, but now, I was ready to graduate from only selling marijuana, ecstasy, and prescription pills, to selling cocaine as well!

Now, I was truly entering dangerous and deadly territory! I recall giving one of my other drug dealing neighbors, who lived just across the pond, about a thousand dollars to buy cocaine for me for the first time. If my first cocaine deal would have gone smoothly, the sky would have been the limit to how much cocaine I would have bought in the days afterwards. My neighbor would act as the middle-man between his supplier and me. It turned out that his supplier ripped him off, and ran away with the money. I wasn't too worried though. I had covered myself by taking his camcorder, expensive luxury watch, and jewelry, as collateral.

Of course, I would have preferred the profits from selling the cocaine. I called him almost every day for the cocaine or a refund of my money, until about a few weeks later, when I went to his apartment. His roommate said that he got busted by the police and moved back home to Maryland, where he was from.

The poor kid... Just like that, his college career and practically, his life was over. I kept hearing stories almost weekly, about students getting busted left and right by confidential informants and undercover cops.

Stella, who was now practically my best friend and occasional sexual partner, kept warning me not to trust people in Bloomington. I could hear her now.

"Don't be so nice and trusting to townies, Mike! I've lived in Bloomington all my life. They'll rat you out!"

I always brushed off her warnings. My clients loved me, and I couldn't imagine any of them betraying me. I thought I was too smart and careful for it to happen to me. I continued to use code name and slang, and would never say the actual drug names on the phone. I remember spending weeks trying to decide a safer and innovative way of saying the names of the laundry list of different drugs that I was dealing, names that no one was using and could be easily construed as non drug related conversations. I thought long and hard. Then one day, I glanced over at the floor in the corner of my bedroom, and there was the answer, just staring at me! It was the case containing the remainder of copied CD's that I had bought and sold door to door, during my freshman year to pay my bills. I had kept the copies just in case someone still wanted to buy them. I was never one to waste products.

One of the CD's that I had copied were by the hip hop rapper, 'DMX'. Another CD was by the rock group, 'Green Day'. I knew I had the perfect idea! I would call the ecstasy, also known as 'x', "DM(X) CD's". And I would call the marijuana, also known as 'green', "(Green)day CD's". That way, if the police ever taped my phone, I could always argue that I was referring to actual CD's. My customers thought it was brilliant.

My precautions didn't end there. One day, I was channel surfing on television, when I noticed an infomercial for a food saving, vacuum sealer machine. The host was raving about how you could save perishable foods for extended periods of time, by putting the food into special heavy duty plastic bags and sealing it, while removing all the air from the bag with the machine. Then the host said that the food inside the vacuum sealed bags would be completely smell proof.

At that instant, I had an epiphany! I got right on the phone and placed an order for the machine. I was going to conceal the aroma of all the marijuana that I had under my bed in those vacuum sealer bags. Plus, I was going to start shipping the drugs through the mail nationally!

Just a few weeks before, I was at a fraternity party when a buddy of mine showed me that he had been shipping psychedelic, hallucinogenic mushrooms, through the mail from a friend in another state, hundreds of miles away. He told me that it was very easy and simple to do, since the postal service didn't thoroughly inspect the mail. I must admit, it was a bit tempting, but I was a little weary. However, when I saw the infomercial for the vacuum food saver machine, all the stars were aligned. All the dots were connected. I was going national!

The day that I received the package with the vacuum food saver in it, I called up a couple of my high school buddies and raved to them about how much money I was making selling drugs, and how much better a quality the marijuana was, compared to the terrible quality marijuana sold in the ghetto. I described the colors, the aroma, the white hairs, the powdery white THC that blanketed the buds of the marijuana, and the stickiness of the buds. They couldn't believe their ears. They had never seen, let alone, heard of anything like that. They were sold! They became extremely excited after hearing my marketing and advertising pitch to them.

Within a week, a handful of my best friends from back home had sent me cash and money orders, worth hundreds of dollars, through the mail. I had custom-made small, vacuum sealed packets, filled with small amounts of marijuana. I put the sealed samples into potato chip bags and resealed the potato chip bags with the vacuum. I remained as calm as possible, but I remember how nervous I was, the first time I went to the post office to ship the packages. If the police had been patiently waiting for the right moment to arrest me, this would be the perfect opportunity. I could be imprisoned for a very long time for national drug trafficking! I pictured undercover agents suddenly coming out of nowhere and arresting me as I exited the post office grounds.

When I drove away, and made it safely back to my apartment, I breathed a huge sigh of relief. But the trial wasn't over. The packages still could have been intercepted in the mail by federal agents and postal workers before arriving at my friends' addresses.

A few days later, to my relief, my friends from back home called me raving about my clever shipping method, the high quality of the marijuana, and how they had never seen or smoked anything like that before. The trial run was a success! They wanted more!

By September of 2002, I had officially become a full-blown national drug dealer! I was selling marijuana. I was selling ecstasy. I was selling prescription pills. I was selling psychedelic mushrooms. And I was selling what I thought to be acid. I was selling almost every major drug, except for cocaine, heroin and methamphetamines.

I always told myself however, that no matter how much money I could make, I would never dream of selling heroin. All the other drugs that I was selling were bad, but I knew that methamphetamines, and especially heroin were the worst, most destructive and harmful drugs anyone could take! I wanted absolutely nothing to do with them! I had enough clients and drugs to deal with.

I treated drug dealing as a 24 hour, 7 day a week business. I always slept with my cell phone next to my ears. 3am...4am...5am... I would answer calls from customers. It didn't matter what time of the day or night it was. My goal was to make as much money, as fast as possible, to pay my tuition and get completely out of the business.

To increase my profits and to add a new product to the market, I learned how to bake brownie treats, brownies that were made with THC content from marijuana.

Soon after, my sales and profits multiplied. Most of my customers had never seen anything like that before. Some customers, including myself, previously thought that brownies that made you high were fictitious, and only in the movies. They were amazed! I soon started shipping the brownies nationally to friends as well, and selling them at parties that I went to. I was doing things that no one else was doing. I was selling thousands of dollars of drugs every single week.

Soon, I began indulging in some of my profits. I threw lavish champagne, Grey Goose, and Belvedere vodka parties. More and more, beautiful girls came into the picture.

Before I knew it, my 19th birthday was days away. I had grown up so fast and been through so much in the past year. I had done things that I never thought I would have ever done. I had lived a life that most 18 year olds could only imagine.

My best friends decided to throw me a birthday party that weekend. I had been contemplating whether or not to try ecstasy (real ecstasy) for my first time on my 19th birthday. It seemed that everyone had already tried ecstasy during their freshman year in college, or in high school and middle school. I saw myself as the only one on campus that had not tried ecstasy before.

During the days leading to my birthday, I built up my excitement to try one of my ecstasy pills that all my customers had been raving about. I convinced myself that I might as well try ecstasy now, under my own free will, just in case someone slipped it into my drink in the future, and I wouldn't be able to handle the foreign and unexpected effects.

The week leading up to my 19th birthday celebration, I asked everyone who had tried ecstasy before, so many questions about how they felt when they took ecstasy, and if they had any negative side-affects or bad experiences. Their descriptions were coinciding. Each detailed description that my friends gave me got me more and more excited, as my birthday approached.

Finally, I had made up my mind that I was going to do it! On my 19th birthday, my friends and I all took ecstasy! I remember waiting patiently and nervously for the effects to kick in. I desperately hoped that I wouldn't have a negative reaction, as I did, when I smoked marijuana for the first time, and ended up lying on the sidewalk at night, thinking that I had died. Another experience like that would have surely been embarrassing.

During the party, a few hours after my friends and I had taken the ecstasy pills, all my friends were feeling the effects. Not me – I felt absolutely nothing. I remember my friends coming up to me every now and then, throughout the party, asking me whether I felt anything. I kept telling them that I didn't feel anything.

It turned out to be a fun night and birthday party, but I wasn't the least bit impressed. Maybe, I had a defective pill. Maybe, my metabolism was too fast to feel the effects. Maybe, because I was naturally always happy, there wasn't a big change in my feelings, emotions, or the chemistry of my body. Whatever the reason was, everyone was experiencing an ecstasy roll, but I on the other hand, hardly felt anything.

Chapter 10

Toward the end of the previous summer, before my second year in Indiana, I met a guy by the name of Connor, who would forever change the course of my life! Connor was a moderately tall, pale skinned, lanky townie, about 18 or 19 years old. He wasn't an Indiana University student, however he lived in a house near campus. By fate, I met Connor in a gas station one day. As usual, I would always ask almost everyone that I met if they smoked marijuana, and then, in an ambiguous and discrete manner, whether they were looking for any drugs. He said he was, as most people I would meet would say. We exchanged contact numbers, and agreed to meet later. I didn't hear from Connor for quite some time after that day.

Then one afternoon, out of the blue, he called me, telling me that he had been in jail for a little over a month, because his uncle or cousin had betrayed him by becoming a drug informant with the Bloomington Police. He said that he had been caught with a relatively small amount of drugs and was given just a few months of house arrest. A red flag immediately went off in my head. I had never dealt with anyone that I had knowledge of being in trouble with the law. Up until then, I had only dealt with close friends and Indiana University students. However, he seemed like a laid back kid. He sounded upfront and genuine on the phone. Plus, I was never one to turn away money, so I followed my instincts, and gave him the benefit of the doubt.

Over the course of the following months, Connor was a constant customer. Just like all my customers, we became good friends. He referred friends to come and buy their drugs from me, and even suggested cheaper suppliers for me to buy my drugs from.

Business was rapidly increasing. I was making more and more money each passing week. I would get a drug shipment in, then immediately, with much excitement, send a mass text message to all my friends and clients. And like clockwork, the calls would instantly start pouring in.

I even started tracking which days and exact times of days were best to buy the shipments of drugs from my suppliers at the most rock bottom prices. I knew the market. I knew when my suppliers were most desperate to sell. And I even discovered the exact times of the day, as well as particular days of the week that I could buy the drugs for the cheapest prices.

Drug dealing became an art to me. And I was good at it – really good at it. I could always command the lowest prices from my suppliers, because I never stayed exclusive to only one supplier. They all knew that I sold out extremely fast, kept bringing them money week after week, and most of all, that I was trustworthy.

Sometimes, I would buy a large shipment, sell out the same hour, and then come right back, knocking on their door, needing to buy more drugs. I was great at what I did. And I knew it! A couple of times, when I ran out of marijuana, and frantically called around, looking for a supplier who had inventory, my client Connor, acted as a middle man, and delivered the marijuana to me. Week after week, month after month, all was well and business as usual.

Then one day, Connor asked me to do him a favor and front him some marijuana until he got paid in a few days.

I said, "Sure..."

Sometimes customers would ask for that favor, and would pay me back on their next purchase. So, without hesitation, I fronted Connor about $40 dollars worth of marijuana. He must have entered into a time where his finances were not so good, because week after week went by, and he could not repay his debt to me. He would always tell me that he would have the money the next day. A few times, he told me to drive over to his house to pick up the money. I would get there, and then he would give me an excuse as to why he didn't have the money.

One time, I was upstairs with him and some of his friends, talking business, when out of nowhere, Connor's probation officer showed up in his apartment. I wasn't too happy that the officer saw me associating with Connor while he was on house arrest, but there was nothing I could do at that point. He had already seen my face. I didn't think much of it after that day. Every now and then, I would call Connor to see if he was able to pay me. Still, he had more excuses. I didn't stress much. It was only $40 dollars. However, I realized very early in my drug dealing days, that when customers owe you money, you lose a lot more potential business from them, as they avoid you, while buying from other drug dealers that they did not owe money to. So, my goal was always to collect the debt as fast as possible, so that they could resume giving me business.

After weeks of owing me money, Connor resumed buying from me again, claiming that his friends gave him the money to buy the drugs from me. I had a feeling that it was his money, and I could have canceled his debt to me by keeping the money and not giving him any drugs in return, but I decided not to cause any tension between us over just $40 dollars.

Then one day, Connor said he knew some friends that could sell me a pound of high quality marijuana for only a few thousand dollars. I rejoiced!

I thought to myself, "This is the big break that I've been looking for!"

I had always heard rumors, that other dealers were buying their drugs from sources that were a lot cheaper than my sources.

"Now," I thought, "I've found the right source!"

Now, I wouldn't have to pay those expensive prices that I had been paying all along. I called my partner and friend, Landon, and told him the exciting news. He was in! I walked around the pond to his apartment and collected his half of the investment, borrowed the keys to his car, and told him I'd be back in just a few hours.

In Landon's old white car that evening, I drove to meet with Connor's friends at the 7eleven convenient store parking lot across from the Eigenmenn dormitory. When I got there, Connor's friends told me that we would be driving quite a way from campus to buy the marijuana from the dealer. Reluctantly and cautiously, I agreed. I called Landon to fill him in on where I was going. Now, Connor's friends and I were on our way.

Into the night, I followed closely behind them, for what seemed to be forever. We drove and drove and drove far away from campus, deep into the boon docks. It was now getting close to midnight.

Finally, after an endless drive, they stopped their car on the side of a dark street in a quiet neighborhood. Then they came to my car and said that we were just a few blocks from the supplier's home, but that they had just spoken to the supplier on the phone, and he didn't want me to know where he lived or see his face.

Immediately, a red flag went off in my head. Connor's friends wanted me to give them the thousands of dollars of Landon's and my money, so that they could buy the marijuana from their connection. I hesitated at first. I didn't know these guys. They could just take Landon's and my money, and I would never see them again. I had a tough decision to make. At first, I told them to bring me a sample first, before I gave them the money. They gave me some excuse about how that would not be possible.

Next, I made a few other suggestions. They had an excuse for each suggestion. I had run out of options. I was basically backed into a corner. I wasn't willing to refuse to give them the money in advance. I had just driven for many miles to get the marijuana. I was not going to return to campus empty handed. I had sold out of my supply, and had so many customers ringing my phone off the hook, and texting me to buy marijuana, even as I drove to the supplier that night. If these prices were real, I would make about double of what I usually made. I had to take a chance!

Besides, "These are Connor's friends." I thought, "They wouldn't steal my money."

Finally, when all else failed, I asked them to give me whatever collateral they had with them. They had nothing but a cheap old watch and a wallet with a driver's license in it. That would have to do. Against my better judgment, I gave Connor's friends about $4000 dollars in cash.

Next, they told me to follow them just a few more blocks in order to find a secluded place to park. As I drove behind their car, they led me to what seemed, under the pitch black night sky, to be a pond or a lake. They assured me not to worry, and said that they would be right back in just a few minutes with the marijuana. I trusted them. I waited and waited by the dark body of water and nearby shack, with absolutely no cell phone reception in that area. I had absolutely no idea where I was. Fifteen minutes went by... They hadn't returned. Thirty minutes went by... Still no show. Forty-five minutes... Still, no one! My patience was quickly running out. I sat there alone in the dark, still giving them the benefit of doubt that they would return. Soon, my optimism turned into uncertainty, and the realization that they were probably not coming back.

Finally, after about an hour and a half of sitting in the car in the middle of nowhere, now, almost midnight, I realized and conceded that I had been hustled. I could not believe it. I had been extremely careful in the past, not to let something like this happen to me. I was furious! I had just lost $4000 dollars of Landon's and my money! I turned the keys in the ignition, started the car, and then attempted to navigate my way back home to campus. I had no idea how to get back home to campus.

Suddenly, about five minutes during the drive, I noticed a car that I could have sworn was Connor's friend's, driving toward me, traveling in the opposite direction. My heart jumped! It was very dark, and there were no street lights, but I was sure it was them!

Maybe, it was in my mind, but I thought I saw the driver and passenger duck their heads down when they saw me. Their car seemed to have sped up as I tried to quickly make a U-turn. I remember searching the area for quite some time, getting even more lost, hungry, frustrated, and tired as I drove.

I finally stopped searching, and decided to head back home. After driving for quite some time, in my attempt to navigate my way back home, I discovered that I had drove for miles in the wrong direction. I was now in trouble! My cell phone's battery life was dying. Even if my cell phone had some battery life, there was absolutely no reception in the area. I also had no money. And now, the gas tank was near empty! I had to think fast and focus! It was only a matter of time that I would be soon stranded in pitch black, in the middle of nowhere, and with no phone service!

Finally, I found a diner and got some decent directions. Soon, I was getting a bit closer to campus, but that was only half the battle. The car began to fail, because of the near empty petroleum tank. But, with sweat forming on my forehead, I kept pushing forward.

Finally, I barely made it back to my best friends, Landon, Gavin, and Gabriel's apartment. I broke the news to them. I felt that I had let Landon down. He trusted me with thousands of dollars of his money, and I had gotten it stolen. He wasn't angry at me though.

Reflecting, it is these types of situations, and many other memories, that make Landon one of my best friends in the world. My friends suspected that Connor was in on the scam. Connor, of course denied that he had anything to do with the theft, when I called him. We had to decide what to do fast! I remember my friends being as upset as I was, and wanting to drive straight to Connor's house with bats and weapons, but I told them that we will figure out another, smarter way to retrieve the stolen money. I always tried to avoid violence, and would rather brainstorm a tactical and sensible plan of action, before irrationally acting.

For now, we would put our troubles behind us, and go out drinking at a party. It's interesting to think about the mindsets of drug dealers. Landon and I had just lost thousands of dollars, and although we were upset, it didn't quite faze us as it would an everyday person who had a normal occupation. Here we were moments later at a party, sipping drinks, flirting with girls, and enjoying ourselves, knowing that we still had thousands of dollars worth of more drugs and cash available to us.

Chapter 11

The following morning, it was back to business as usual. Recounting the series of events in my head, I thought to myself, "So, now Connor has owed me about $40 dollars for weeks now, and his friends just hustled Landon and me out of thousands of dollars." I stayed on Connor, and kept calling his phone for days. I even drove over to his house a couple of times.

Sometimes, no one would answer the door. Other times, his phone would be disconnected. Maybe that was the plan – to get me broke and desperate for money.

Then one fateful night in November, about a week before Thanksgiving holiday, I was hanging out across the pond of my apartment, at the crew, Landon, Gavin, and Gabriel's apartment.

Suddenly, I heard the ever too familiar sound of the special siren ring tone that I had programmed exclusively for my clients. As usual, money popped up in my head, and I'm sure in the crew's minds as well. They had gotten so used to that siren ring tone by now. It was Connor! He called saying that he needed to buy about 260 'DMX CDs', the code word I had told all my customers to use, when they wanted to buy ecstasy from me.

Immediately, I felt a huge wave of excitement and nervousness rush into my chest at the same time! I told Connor that I would find out if I could get it, and would call him back in a few minutes. I became immensely excited! This was my big break that I had been looking for, for so long! Plus, Connor said in code that his friend was willing to pay over $12.50 cents per pill! This was going to be my biggest, most profitable single sale thus far! I was going to negotiate with my supplier to buy the ecstasy for $4 dollars or $5 dollars each.

I was very surprised that he agreed to sell them for so cheap, since I could individually sell them at retail, for up to $35 dollars, and even $40 dollars to certain customers. That would be about a 1000% profit, in a relatively short amount of time! And the funny thing is that I always bargained and pleaded to my suppliers to get even lower prices, telling them that I couldn't make any money at the prices they were giving me. And they believed me because they, themselves, could only sell individual ecstasy pills to their customers for about $10 dollars, retail.

Or, perhaps, I was the fool. And perhaps, they were getting the ecstasy pills for only $1 dollar, or even .50 cents each, and making over 1000% in profits from me. I do recall, that when my main ecstasy supplier was sold out, and his suppliers weren't around, he was only willing to pay $1 dollar per ecstasy pill from me, when I had inventory. However, he was, at first willing to pay up to $5 dollars each. Perhaps, like all commodities, drug prices fluctuate up and down. Or maybe, just as I did years later, he became enlightened of the true wholesale cost of buying mass amounts of ecstasy pills.

Nevertheless, I did not really care at the time. As long as I was making a lot of profit on my end, I was happy. I immediately called my supplier to buy the 260 'DMX pills' from him. I could tell by the tone of his voice, and his speech pattern, that I had caught him by surprise. He told me that he only had about 150 pills left. I could sense that he was a bit suspicious, since I had only bought about 50 to 60 ecstasy pills at a time from him in the past. And now, I was asking for over two and a half jars. A 'jar' is slang for 100 ecstasy tablets. And a 'boat' is the slang for 1000 ecstasy tablets. I couldn't fathom actually buying a boat at the time. It was beyond my imagination back then.

My supplier, who Landon had introduced me to in the beginning of the year, immediately called Landon after hanging up with me, to find out whether he would vouch for me, wanting to know whether Landon thought anything was suspicious. Landon, who was sitting right next to me, when his friend, our supplier called, gave him the green light, and told him that I was in the apartment with him when Connor called.

The next day, Landon and I drove over to our supplier's apartment to buy the ecstasy pills. As soon as I had the drugs in hand, I called Connor. He told me to give him a bit more time to get the money together, and would have it all in a day or two, just a few days before Thanksgiving Day.

Time was of the essence. I had planned on going to my best friend and fellow wrestling teammate, Gabriel's parents' home, in Illinois, on Thanksgiving Eve. I had planned on buying the ecstasy pills from my supplier and then immediately selling them to Connor. I didn't like having to hold on to that many pills in my apartment. The delays were making me begin to think that he could not really get all that money. I began to worry. But then, I thought to myself, "Hey, I could always sell out as soon as the students come back from the holiday break." Plus, I would take about 20 or so pills to Illinois with Gabriel, and make a few hundred dollars while on vacation.

Looking back, it was a very inconsiderate, risky, and irresponsible thought to take the ecstasy pills to Gabriel's parents' house. Anything could have happened, and poor Gabriel's family would have been dragged into jeopardy. But by then, I thought I was untouchable, and couldn't be caught. How the next series of events proved otherwise!

Finally, the night before we were set to leave to Illinois, Connor called, saying that he had all the money, and would be at my condo, first thing, the following morning. I made sure that I told him that I was going on a road trip to Illinois, and that I would not be in town for about a week, so he should not be late.

I remember the following morning like it was yesterday. Gabriel and I were texting and calling each other, cracking jokes as usual. We were extremely excited about going on vacation, and the mischief we would be getting into while in Illinois. Connor called me a few times to follow up with me, letting me know that he was on his way, and not to leave yet. He asked me to stall the person who was driving Gabriel and me to Illinois.

As usual, I hadn't started packing a thing, until last minute, so I was laying out about a dozen outfits on my bed that I would be wearing for the only four or five days that we would be vacationing in Illinois. I was doing some last minute counting and recounting, making sure that all the ecstasy tablets were neatly and perfectly packed. I was making sure that my other drugs – the psychedelic mushrooms, the acid sugar cubes, the marijuana, and the prescription pills, plus, the thousands of dollars that I had saved, were safely hidden in my secret stash.

Finally, about 30 minutes before our scheduled departure to Illinois, I received a call from Connor, saying that he was just a few blocks away, in the Kroger grocery store parking lot. He assured me that he would be at my place shortly.

It was show time!

Now, although I had dealt with Connor numerous times before, for some reason, my instincts told me to take extra precautions that I had never taken before, on this particular drug transaction. I trusted him to a degree, however, when you are doing the biggest deal that you have ever done so far, and the thought of going to jail for a very, very long time comes to mind, you take a few radical and unconventional steps.

As I said before, I had read and researched any and all possible drug related stories and news articles that I could get my hands on, on the internet. So a few minutes before Connor arrived at my door, a story flashed in my head, of a man being acquitted of drug dealing because his life and family were threatened to be killed, unless he committed the crime. Actually, I'm not sure if the crime was drug related. It's possible that the crime was not drug related, but a crime, nonetheless.

I did some quick thinking, and got out a yellow Post-it paper out of my desk and wrote, in big letters: READ THIS OUT LOUD! "Sell me 160 ecstasy pills or I'll kill you and your family!"

"That's not enough..." I thought to myself.

I couldn't afford to take any chances. So, just minutes before Connor pulled into my apartment complex, I neatly placed all the drugs in an inconspicuous plastic Kroger shopping bag, tied the plastic bag up, and then threw the bag outside on the floor, about ten feet away from my apartment door.

I remember thinking, "He had better come quickly."

I was imagining a random person just walking by my apartment and picking up the bag, then walking off with my drugs. Or even worse, a rodent, like a squirrel, raccoon, or a skunk smelling the drugs in the Kroger bag and running off with all of my investment. I remember nervously opening the door to check on the bag almost every thirty seconds, hoping that Connor would hurry up and come already.

I finally heard a knock on my door. I looked through the peep hole in the door. It was Connor! I opened the door, allowed him into my apartment, and gave him a handshake hug, then immediately held up to his face, the yellow Post-it note, that had written in big bold letters: READ THIS OUT LOUD! "Sell me 160 ecstasy pills or I'll kill you and your family!"

He immediately had a shocked and confused look on his face. This was something completely new to him. We had never gone through this procedure before. But I looked him in the eyes, pointed my finger at the note, and nodded my head, giving him a signal to read the note aloud. After a quick pause, he read the note out loud.

I thought to myself, "If he is wearing a wire, I am covered."

Next, he even voluntarily lifted up his sweatshirt quickly, exposing his chest and stomach, to reassure me that he was trustworthy and that he wasn't wearing a wire. Phase one was complete. I felt a bit more secure and comfortable around him after that.

Next, I reopened my apartment door. We walked outside into the cold about five feet from the apartment door. I remember Connor having such a confused look on his face. As we walked and got to the plastic bag, I inconspicuously and quickly signaled for him to pick up the plastic bag. The confused and bewildered look on his face only grew stronger. He bent down, picked up the bag, then looked around nervously into the distance, scanning all directions, as if he knew or thought that someone was watching us. Perhaps, he was beginning to think that I was an informant or an undercover police officer that was setting him up.

We proceeded back into the warmth of my apartment. I knew that if he himself was an undercover cop or an informant, he couldn't say that I sold or gave him any drugs, even after he made the threat on my life and my family's lives. I could always have an attorney argue that he found a plastic bag of drugs outside. Plus, it wasn't as if I myself picked up the bag of drugs and handed it to him. I rationalized to myself that, just as if two friends were at a nightclub, party, or walking down the street would find a small bag of marijuana or an ecstasy pill on the floor, then one friend picked it up, that wouldn't mean that it was a drug dealing transaction.

Albeit, this bag was filled with a much larger amount of drugs, but the principle still applied, I imagined. We reentered my apartment, and then I made another gesture with my right index finger pressed against my lips, signaling Connor to keep quiet, and to not say anything. I was in total control of how I wanted this transaction to play out.

Next, I signaled for him to open the bag. He slowly opened the plastic bag and discovered the ecstasy pills neatly packaged tightly into groups of about ten, in small baggies. Those baggies were all perfectly placed in a sandwich-sized Ziploc bag. I've always been a perfectionist. I would always package my drugs neatly and organized for my customers. I'm sure that my perfectionism gave me an advantage over my competitors. I highly doubt that other drug dealers paid attention to the little details as I did. Whenever my customers would come over to my apartment, they had no worries. I made them feel at home. They felt comfortable, and they knew that the deal would be fast, safe, friendly, and professional.

After Connor and I counted the pills together, and confirmed that everything was there, he gave me the $2000 dollars. In front of him, I counted, and double counted the money. Everything was there. Even with all the extra precautions that I had taken, I remember carefully looking at the bills as I counted, to see if police had put any markings on the bills. I had watched a bunch of movies, and heard so many stories of how police officers would put inconspicuous marks on 'buy money', in order to prove that the dealer accepted money in exchange for drugs. If I was arrested, and any unmarked currency was seized from my apartment, an attorney representing me could simply argue that I had been saving that money for a long time.

We were all set! The deal was done! I had the money, and he had the drugs. As routine, he then took a few of the pills out of the baggies, just to examine them, by tasting a few tablets with the tip of his tongue. I never really understood why people did that with ecstasy. I could understand when people tasted cocaine with the tips of their tongues, since cocaine has a distinct cocoa leaf taste. But I guess the common conception was, that putting ecstasy on the tip of your tongue gives your tongue a slight shock if the tablet was made with genuine MDNA(3,4-Methylenedioxymethamphetamine), the chemical term for ecstasy.

I'm almost certain that doing so is a misconception, but if it made my buyers feel more comfortable, then I wasn't going to stop them. After tasting a few tablets, he asked me what kind of ecstasy pills they were, since I was selling him two different kinds of pills. Half of the pills were white, and had a stamped logo of clogs. You know, the types of heavy, usually wooden-soled shoes that is worn in the Netherlands. The other half of the ecstasy pills were blue, stamped with a Mercedes-Benz logo.

Not suspecting anything, I quietly replied, "Clogs and blue Mercedes-Benz."

So, that was it. He put the pills back into the baggie, put all the baggies containing ten to twelve pills in each, into the Ziploc sandwich bag, and then placed the Ziploc sandwich bag into the Kroger plastic bag. He then tied up the plastic bag and stuffed it into the interior pocket of his jacket. I noticed that he kept a baggie of about ten tablets for himself, which he stuffed into his underwear. I smiled slightly and shook my head, because I knew that he was going to tell his buyer that he could only get 150 pills, instead of 160 pills at the $2000 dollar price. I had seen so many middle-men and delivery boys, who bought from me do that in the past, so it wasn't a surprise. I couldn't blame them. No one wants to do all that leg work, and take all that risk of trafficking drugs for free.

He said he would ingest a few of the pills over the Thanksgiving holiday weekend, and save the rest for later. As he was getting ready to leave, I offered him a snack and something to drink, but he declined, saying that he had to get going. Before I opened the door to let him out, I told him to have a safe Thanksgiving holiday, and to be careful while driving back with the drugs. He replied with what seemed to be a sincere "thanks".

He had mentioned that he was getting off of house arrest and probation in a few days, and said that we should definitely hang out when I got back to campus from Illinois. I was happy for him. He had really helped me out with this purchase. He actually came through, and almost made up for his dishonest friends ripping me off weeks before. When I saw that he was all set, and had the drugs securely concealed under his jacket, I got the door for him, shook hands, and hugged, then said "good bye".

The second I closed my apartment door, I rejoiced and pumped my fist in celebration. Another successful transaction!

Then, immediately, it was back to business! I went into my usual speed routine that I had, right after a customer left my apartment. I sprinted to my bathroom, ripped up the yellow Post-it note, with the death threat written on it, that I had instructed Connor to read out loud, and then quickly flushed all the pieces down the toilet. I had always had the vision of movies, when police officers stormed into a home, immediately after a drug deal. So, immediately after most of my deals, especially large deals, I would quickly race to destroy or conceal any evidence in sight. I never took any chances.

Next, I stashed the $2000 dollars that Connor had paid me into a secret stash safe in the corner of my closet. They were safes disguised as coffee cans and soda bottles that I had bought online earlier that year. No one would have ever suspected that in those containers, surrounded by real cans of food, were thousands of dollars of cash and drugs.

Once all the evidence was destroyed and hidden, I proceeded to packing my clothes. Gabriel had sent me a text message while Connor was in my apartment, letting me know that he would be ready in a few moments. I was as excited as ever to go on the road trip to Illinois and see Gabriel's amazing family again.

Then suddenly, a fateful authoritative and loud knock on my apartment door forever altered the course of my journey in life!

"Is Gabriel here already?" I thought to myself.

"Coming..." I said, as I curiously walked to the door.

When I looked into the peephole of the door, I saw two bulky men with uniforms on! It's strange, the absolute first thought that entered my mind was that it was one of the workers of my apartment complex's maintenance department. I thought that they just came to do some last minute inspections on my apartment before I left for the holiday.

Perhaps, my mind was already on the forthcoming vacation and the fact that I had just made about $1000 dollars profit in a matter of minutes. But, for whatever the reason, I didn't pay attention to what kind of dark blue uniforms the men were wearing.

"Who is it?" I asked calmly, as I looked into the peephole. "Bloomington Police... Open Up!" one officer answered in a tranquil, yet authoritative manner.

Only then, through the peephole of my door, did their badges and police uniforms become apparent to me.

It's amazing, all that time of drug dealing, I had always mentally prepared myself to have some sort of elaborate escape if the police ever raided or showed up at my apartment. I had always pictured myself sprinting to my drug stashes in my apartment and flushing large amounts of drugs down the toilet.

Then, I saw myself frantically escaping through a back door or window. That's the way I envisioned it playing out. What happened when the Bloomington Police showed up at my door was the exact opposite. The best description of how I felt was: numb and calm – almost like it wasn't happening in real time.

Absolutely nothing went through my mind after the men declared who they were. My mind was completely blank for those few seconds. I didn't think about any lies that I would tell them once I opened the door. I didn't think of Connor betraying me. I didn't think of going to jail for a very long time. I simply took a deep breath, braced myself, opened my apartment door, and then let them in.

For some time, I had wondered why the police officers chose to knock on my door, instead of kicking my door in. I could have had ample time to flush all my drugs down the toilet and escaped through my living room patio door or through my room window.

Even worse, I could have been armed with a gun, and came out with a blaze of bullets. Maybe, Connor had previously described my peaceful character to them. Maybe, they knew that I had nowhere to run to, even if I escaped. Or maybe, they didn't know the extent of my business and how much drugs and cash that I still had cleverly hidden in my apartment.

"You're under arrest for drug dealing..." one officer said.

The party was over for me! My time had finally come! My life would never be the same from then on!

One of the officers instructed me to put my hands behind my head. I cooperatively complied. I felt the cold, hard, carbon steel handcuffs tighten around my strong wrists. The feeling of the moment was just surreal. I was actually getting arrested for drug dealing. All those movies and stories that I had heard of, and never truly grasped that they were real, was literally unfolding in real time before my eyes.

Within seconds of being handcuffed, I snapped back into the moment. Oddly, the first and only thing that came to mind, was that I wouldn't be able to go to Illinois with Gabriel for Thanksgiving. I could just see the look of shock and awe on Gabriel's face when he finds out that I've been arrested. The first thing they continued to ask me from the moment they entered my door was, who is my supplier.

"Who's your supplier?" they repeated, over and over again. "We just want the 'big fish'..." "This is how it works." they continued, attempting to convince me, "First we get the little fish, then we get the big fish. We don't want you. We just want the 'big fish'."

Remembering the plan that I had rehearsed over and over in my head, if I ever got caught, I said very little to the police.

"I don't know what you are talking about." I calmly answered.

"We have you on a wire selling ecstasy to an informant." one officer immediately responded.

They never mentioned Connor's name, however they made it clearly obvious that Connor was their informant. It wasn't a coincidence that they came to arrest me minutes after Connor had left my apartment. I acted absolutely clueless. The officers continued.

"Do you want to go to jail, or do you want to go free?"
"Wow." I thought to myself.

I had heard these lines in movies so many times, and now I was hearing them in real life. I literally felt as if I was in a scene from a movie. In retrospect, they made it seem as if, if I would have told them who my supplier was, and worn a wire in a controlled buy for them, then I would have no legal problems afterwards – that I would be free to go as if my arrest never happened. That is how I understood it at the time. I'm thankful, however, that my heart wouldn't allow me to betray a friend, or even an enemy for that matter.

"I have no idea what you're talking about." I repeated, as other officers began to search my apartment.

Interestingly, still, the only thing on my mind was how disappointed Gabriel was going to be that I had been arrested.

"Can I please just call my friend, and tell him that I won't be going to Illinois with him?" I asked over and over again.

"What's your friend's name?"

"Gabriel." I answered.

I remember laughing in my head when they began to think that innocent Gabriel was the big drug lord that I was getting my drugs from.

"Is this Gabriel guy your supplier?" I laughed and shook my head.

"Poor Gabriel." I thought to myself, "Now the Bloomington Police Department thinks he's a big time drug lord."

"No." I replied, "He's just my best friend. Can I just call him please?" Suddenly, Gabriel called to tell me that our ride was ready. They finally agreed to let me tell Gabriel that I had been arrested, and that I would not be joining him for the Thanksgiving holiday. They immediately sent a couple of officers across the pond to search my best friends Gabriel, Landon, and Gavin's apartment. As I had imagined, Gabriel was completely caught by surprise. He had just spoken to me minutes earlier, excited about the trip, and now, I was going to jail.

After the police handcuffed me, they asked me if I had any weapons in my pocket. "No... I don't." I responded, with an almost insulted look on my face. "What kind of person did they take me for?" I thought to myself, not knowing that that was a standard question they asked. "Why would I carry a weapon?" I thought.

Throughout my dealings, I thought of myself not as a typical drug dealer, but as a sophisticated, nicely dressed, and educated dealer.

With my hands securely cuffed behind my body, an officer proceeded to search my pockets. I remember exactly what I had on that afternoon. I was wearing black boots, some Marithé Françio Girbaud denim jeans, with numerous pockets, and a warm red, Polo Ralph Lauren knitted sweatshirt, worn under a black, cowhide leather jacket. Pocket after pocket, the officer emptied my pockets, finding my cell phone and wallet.

And then finally, he searched one of the pockets in my pants that were near my knees. What he pulled out was a stack of money neatly wrapped with a rubber band. I had about $2000 dollars in my pocket. That was going to be the first time I was finally going to start a college tuition savings fund. I had planned on taking those $2000 odd dollars to the post office and getting a money order, then immediately shipping the money order to my mom that day, to start a bank account for me. I knew she would wonder and ask me where the money came from, but I always told her that I was doing business. I calculated that I could send about $1000 dollars a week, thereafter. At that pace, my dream of paying for my tuition would finally come true. It would have been a big accomplishment for me to finally set up that college tuition savings fund.

The officers awkwardly examined the money with a puzzled and confused look on their faces. That wasn't the $2000 odd dollars that they had photocopied the serial numbers of at the police station, in order to use as evidence to convict me in court. Although I wasn't out of the forest yet, The Lord had stepped in, in a major way and saved me once again!

Fatefully, minutes before Connor came into my apartment, I wrapped my own $2000 odd dollars in a rubber band and put it into my pocket. So, when Connor gave me the photocopied buy-money, I immediately put it into my secret stash safe. If I was not so eager and excited to immediately take the steps in setting up my college tuition savings fund, and had decided to just wait until I get Connor's payment, the police would have one additional, very strong piece of evidence to use against me in court.

Still puzzled and confused, the officers examined the money further. "This isn't the buy-money..." one officer said in dismay. "Where's the buy-money that you just received?"

Once again, I said, "I have no idea what you're talking about officer." The officers had been surveilling my apartment complex throughout the entire deal, and noticed that a former Indiana University football player, who lived in the apartment above me, had drove out of the complex shortly after the drug transaction between Connor and me. They thought that he was my partner, and that I had somehow given him the money just before they came to my door.

At this point, the police officers were quite frustrated. The buy-money was one of the key evidences that they would need to convict me in court. And now, to their knowledge, they had just watched it drive away. Not saying a word, I allowed them believe that. Little did they know that the money was safely concealed within inches of where they were searching. I knew that if they thought that the money was gone, then they wouldn't look so diligently to find the buy-money in my apartment.

I stood there watching, as the police officers emptied bags of sugar into my kitchen sink. They searched my refrigerator and freezer, looking to see if, like most drug dealers, I had hidden any money or drugs in there. They found nothing but frozen steak, grilled chicken, and vegetables. From the living room where I stood handcuffed, I listened nervously, as another team of officers searched my bedroom. They searched the bathroom inside my bedroom. They searched under my bed. They searched my closet, where the fake coffee can safe stashes were mixed with real canned goods. I thought for sure, that they would recognize the safe stashes as fakes, compared to the actual canned goods that surrounded them. They didn't suspect a thing. It looked like my secret hiding place was a clever and brilliant idea!

So far, they had absolutely no physical evidence to use in court, but the blue digital scale with barely any THC, marijuana residue that they had found in my front pocket of my pants. But they needed far more than a digital scale to convict me in court. They radioed other police officers to quickly find the former IU football player and search his car, but as far as they were concerned, the buy-money was as good as gone.

Soon, they began overturning my living room furniture and cutting open the bottom linings of my sofas, thinking that I could have hidden the money or more drugs in there.

Once again, they found nothing. My former roommate, Dylan's room was locked as standard procedure by the apartment complex management after he moved out. They asked me where the key for the second bedroom was.

Apparently, they thought that I had both bedrooms for myself.

"I don't have the key." I answered, pretending to be nervous, in order to get them excited that perhaps, the locked room was full of endless piles of drugs and money.

I must say, I was enjoying fooling them and leading them to false hopes. Anything to take their minds off finding the thousands of dollars, including their buy-money and the variety of other illegal drugs that was hidden in my room, including psychedelic mushrooms, prescription pills, and what I was under the impression were acid sugar cubes. I could see the eager and excited looks on their faces, when I pretended to hesitate, after they asked me whether there were any drugs or weapons in the locked bedroom.

Finally, they decided to kick the door open. By the looks in their eyes, they must have thought that they would discover a room filled with marijuana plants, piles of cocaine, stacks of money, machine guns, AK-47s, and expensive luxury goods, just like in the movies. They must have imagined that this would be the drug bust of their careers.

Boom! A loud noise sounded off, as an officer kicked the door in. What mysteries did they discover in the second bedroom...? Nothing! Just an absolutely empty, cold bedroom... I could see the looks of eager hope and anticipation die down from their faces and instantly turn into looks of disappointment and frustration. I laughed inside my mind.

Finally, after a few more unsuccessful attempts to convince me to reveal to them, who my supplier was, a few officers escorted me to the police car, while the other officers stayed behind for a bit longer. I sat in the back seat of the police car on the way to the station in that ever too familiar, laying on my side position. It had been so many years since I had been arrested and been put in a police car for stealing from the mall in Livingston, New Jersey.

Now, I was arrested for a much greater offense in Bloomington, Indiana.

"How did I end up here?" I asked myself.

So much went through my mind, however, this time, I didn't cry as I did as a child in New Jersey. I just laid there numb, handcuffed, on my side, awaiting my uncertain fate.

Chapter 12

When I arrived at the police station, I was fingerprinted and had my mug shot taken. My emotions ran wild. During my fingerprinting was when the brevity and seriousness of what was unfolding before my eyes hit me. I was officially in the computer system as a criminal. I had to keep my emotions under control. I didn't want to seem timid in front of the unexpectedly pleasant spirited officer who was filing me into the system.

The entire procedure was surreal. I recall having to fill out a questionnaire, asking me multiple questions like, "Have you ever been suicidal?" and other questions like, "Do you have any diseases or viruses?" I was living out a very bad dream! I was then placed into a small, bedroom-sized room with a handful of other men that had been arrested that day. They seemed like good men who just made wrong decisions, but I knew that I definitely did not belong there. I believe I was the only one there who had never been placed in a holding room before. I could not imagine the thought of being put in jail with the rest of the criminal population.

I still had hope. I was allowed to call someone to bail me out. My bail was set at $20,000 dollars. That means that whoever bailed me out would have to pay a 10% bond, $2,000 dollars. The police had confiscated my cell phone for evidence at the time of my arrest. Moments such as these are when you realize that you don't have your friends' and family members' telephone numbers memorized. Not that I would have even dreamt of calling my parents or siblings to tell them that I had been arrested. The only number that I knew by heart was Stella's, my absolute best friend. As I dialed, I wondered how she would handle the shocking and unfortunate news of my untimely arrest.

As I expected, she was devastated! I tried my best to stop her from crying as I spoke to her on the phone. She really loved, and was in love with me. If I never knew before that day, I was certain now. I asked her to come to the police station and quickly bail me out before they transferred me out of the holding room and into the jail with the rest of the prison population. I assured her that I would pay her back immediately after I was released.

My time was quickly running out. I listened to Stella apologizing and crying on the opposite end of the phone, as she told me that she didn't have enough money to bail me out on her own. She was short of breath and seemed to be hyperventilating and having a panic attack on the other end of the phone. Her fears and warnings of me getting arrested had come true.

"Calm down Stella." I said to her, "It's going to be OK."

She certainly didn't expect to come home from her college and hear this shocking news. I pleaded with her to find a way to come up with the money to bail me out. I told her that I would try to call her back later to see if she was able to get the bond money.

Fortunately, the officer was willing to allow me to call her again. About a half an hour later, I was allowed to call Stella again.

"Maubrey," she cried, "I'm so sorry. I can't get that kind of money!"

I was now in a very big predicament. The only other option would be to tell her to go to my apartment and get the money out of my secret safe stash. But I knew that if I told her where the money was, then the police would have gone to my apartment before she arrived. So, I asked the booking officer if I could be allowed to make another call to Stella after the call that I was currently in the middle of with Stella. He agreed. So, I told Stella to drive to my apartment, and I would call her within a few minutes when she arrived.

The police, I'm almost certain, were secretly on another line, listening to the conversation that Stella and I were having. And even if they weren't, the booking officer was sitting right there, listening to our entire conversation. He knew what I was planning on doing.

Shortly after I got off the phone with Stella, I called her again. She was inside my apartment. I was relieved! Now, all I had to do was to instruct her in ambiguous code language and slang, to find the money.

"Look in the closet. It's in there!" I exclaimed repeatedly in frustration. "I don't see any money...!" she cried in equal frustration.

No one knew about those secret safe stashes, surrounded by other canned vegetable goods. I could imagine Stella just discarding them to the side as she vigorously searched for the money.

"I can't find any money!" she repeated.

I tried my best to tell Stella in so many different discrete ways that the money was in the cans. But she couldn't find the money. Had the police officers raced to my apartment for a second time without a warrant, and found the money and drugs in my safes? Perhaps, I may never know. But most likely, that was the case.

My time was now up. With all my friends and clients gone for the Thanksgiving holiday, it looked like I would be spending at least a week in jail! My heart sank to my stomach! I thanked Stella for trying, told her that I loved her, and encouraged her to stay strong until the rest of my best friends, Gavin, Landon, and Gabriel got back to campus. Then I hung up the phone.

I was now on my own! Soon, my street clothes were taken away, and I was forced to take the standard cold shower in front of the booking officer. It was a bit degrading. A supervised shower was mandatory, I learned, in order to prevent any diseases or concealed drugs from entering the jail. I was given a bright orange colored prison uniform to wear, a foam mat to sleep on, and a blanket and a pillow to take to the cell block.

Around midnight, while the other prisoners were fast asleep, I was transported upstairs to the cell block. I was now officially a prisoner of the state of Indiana! The prison was highly over crowded, so I didn't have a jail cell. I had to sleep on the floor. I remember making my bed in a small secluded corner, directly underneath a staircase of the two level cell block. There were about a half a dozen other inmates sleeping on the jail floor. It had been a long and exhausting day for me. I was ready to fall asleep. I rested my head on my pillow, took a deep breath, closed my eyes, and fell into a deep sleep.

Chapter 13

I'll never forget how I felt, when I awoke the following morning. I squinted my eyes as the bright glare of the prison lights shined into my pupils. At first, I had no idea where I was. I thought that my getting arrested and going to jail had all just been a terrible dream. But no, this was no dream. This was real! I quickly realized where I was. I was in jail! I vividly remember the sore, dry feeling in the back of my throat. It hurt so badly when I tried to swallow my saliva. I hadn't eaten in about 24 hours. They were serving corn dogs on the day of my arrest.

"How low and degrading..." I thought to myself.

Before my arrest, I had accustomed myself to eating the finest foods like shrimp, steak, fettuccine, grilled chicken, and lobster. I had never eaten a corn dog before, and there was no way that I was going to eat it now. I refused the meal, confident that I would not have to spend the night in jail.

I was certainly wrong. We had to wake up at about five o'clock in the morning to eat breakfast. We had no option. If you didn't wake up on time, you would miss breakfast that day. I can't forget how miserable I felt waiting in the long line in my orange prison uniform with my food tray in my hand. With my shoulders back and my chest up, I quietly scanned the cell block. I was thinking about how I had seen this depressing scene in so many movies in the past. And now, I was living it.

I remained calm, quiet, and reserved as I ate at a table with a group of inmates. I struggled to eat the prison food. It hurt the back of my throat just to swallow the food and drink. Immediately after breakfast, I went right back to my corner mat underneath the staircase and went right back to sleep.

After a few hours, I woke up again. A few inmates asked me what my name was. And within a few minutes, they brought me a local Bloomington newspaper, showing me that my name was in the paper for being arrested for drug dealing. I was surprised. I couldn't believe that my name was out there in plain view for the entire town to know that I had been arrested for dealing ecstasy. I was surprised, but I wasn't upset. In a way, it actually increased my pride, and made me feel infamous. The inmates were immediately gravitated to me. I could tell that they had respect for me, just because they knew that I was a major drug dealer.

When you're a major drug dealer in jail, you have an immediate advantage. Virtually every prisoner wants to be your friend. Virtually every prisoner wants to know how you got your drugs, and how they can make money with you when they get out of jail. They asked me a lot of questions. I conversed with them, without going into specific details. I had heard many stories of how prisoners were convicted simply by talking too much in jail. They understood and respected my reservation.

After a few days in jail, I was beginning to realize that these people were actually good human beings, who just made wrong decisions in life. They weren't bad people. Before long, I developed bonds with nearly every prisoner in that cell block. I understood them. And they understood me too. When they found out that I was an Indiana University wrestler, they loved and respected me even more. The feeling was definitely mutual.

However, the days seemed endless. Day after day after day, I was talking to Stella on the phone, trying to get her to gather about $2,000 dollars from friends to bail me out. There was a lot of pressure on Stella, but she was trying daily to raise the money to bail me out. I never left her thoughts.

Yes, I could have asked her to call my parents, but there was no way that I was going to do that! I wouldn't dream of letting them know that their son, who was supposed to be studying medicine and getting a college education, was a drug dealer, and had gotten arrested. I was sure that they would be extremely upset and disappointed. Also, I was sure that they would have let me stay in jail to teach me a lesson. I could now hear the phrase that my father would always tell us kids when we were growing up.

"If you ever get in trouble, don't call me!"

I was now in big trouble, and I was not going to call him. I was on my own, as far as letting my parents know was concerned. If I could, I was going to take this arrest to the grave, without ever telling my family. I was too ashamed.

As the days came and went, I was becoming extremely restless. I had to get out! I would never let myself get complacent and comfortable in that prison. There were a few times, that beds in the prison room cells became available, and I was next on the list to get a room, but I requested to continue sleeping on the floor, underneath the stairs. I had now been in jail for about a week. I had spent my first Thanksgiving Day in jail, and far away from my friends and family.

My faith and hopeful optimism was truly being put to the test. The only thing I could do to keep my sanity was read and workout. And soon, I began to draw sketches.

There wasn't a day that went by that I didn't think about Stella. It took an event like this to make me realize how much I loved this girl. And more importantly, how much this girl truly loved me and would do anything for me. Stella wrote me thoughtful letters in jail, cried for me on the phone and in private, and was doing all that she could possibly do to bring me back home. Her actions truly amazed me as I sat in jail. Never did I dream that someone would go through this jeopardy for my sake. She was my angel sent from God! I will always love her for that.

It's amazing to think that at this very moment, as I write this book in a small library in Belleville, NJ, today is the eve of Thanksgiving, exactly seven years since my life had been forever changed. I've come a long way on my journey of life. Seven years ago on this day, I was sitting restlessly in jail. Because of this, every Thanksgiving holiday has an extra special meaning to me. It's an anniversary of the time period that began the transformation of my life!

While in jail, I was given a state appointed public defender. Although I could not afford a private attorney, I felt blessed because I was told that he was the most experienced and seasoned public defender in town. He was an older gentleman in his late fifties to mid sixties. I believed that if anyone could help me, it would be him.

I soon learned that I would need all the help that I could get. I was charged with numerous counts, including selling ecstasy, possession with the attempt to sell the supposed LSD sugar cubes that they found when they rushed to my apartment the second time, and other charges like maintaining a common nuisance. I was in the most devastating position that I had ever been in my short nineteen years on earth. I was facing 60 years in prison if convicted! My heart sank when I first found out the report. There was a possibility that I would die a prisoner for the foolish actions that I had committed. There was no way I could survive 60 years, 30 years, one year, or even one more week in jail, I thought. The only thing keeping me going was Christ and the thought that Stella and my other best friends would be able to come up with the funds to bail me out.

There is no way to accurately describe the terrible feeling of being in jail, especially for the first time. You have absolutely no freedom. It can be quite depressing, if you let it get to you. I tried my best to stay strong and hopeful. At that point, the only thing on my mind was to be bailed out as soon as possible. This place was surely not for me. This was not my life. And in my mind, I knew that after I was set free, there was no way that I would ever return.

Day after day, I witnessed fellow prisoners getting bailed out. In a way, it encouraged me, and made me believe that my time was soon.

Finally, about a week after my arrest, my best friends had returned to campus from Thanksgiving holiday. I remember how happy and thankful I was when I heard the police guard mention my name, that I had visitors. During my brief meeting with Stella and my other best friends, speaking to them behind a bullet proof, two inch thick glass, I tried my best to stay strong and cheerful in their presence. We had a few laughs; I thanked them so much for taking the time to come to visit me. They assured me that they would do everything that they could to raise the $2000 plus dollars to bail me out. Words can't describe how good I felt when they came to visit me in jail. More and more, I knew that they were my true friends. The Lord Jesus has truly blessed me in all my years. And He continues to show His majesty even to this day!

Just a few days ago, I received an unexpected and supernatural blessing. I received a voicemail from my absolute best friend from high school, Benjamin Davis – the one that I spoke of, earlier in the story. The one that he and I were virtually inseparable friends in high school. The one that was like a twin brother. The one that we parted on not so good terms, simply because of money. After almost 10 years of not hearing from or seeing him, The Lord has brought him back into my life. His funny voice mail took me back to the good old days that we had together. Only Christ knows how he was able to get my home number. He was calling from an international number. In the voice mail he gave me his email address to contact him.

Meaning to send Benjamin an email when I had the time, I recall listening to his voice mail a few times with a reminiscent smile on my face over the past few days since he called last week. And then, just two days ago, on Thanksgiving Day, the day that we celebrate and give thanks to old and new friendships from The Lord above, I received an international call. It was my dear old companion, Benjamin. He was calling all the way from Kuwait, in the Middle East. The Lord had showed His all powerful wondrous and awesome works to me once more! Only The Lord can cause a dear friend, separated for a decade, to reconnect through the wire, from half way around the world. We conversed and caught up on good times. He testified of how successful and happy The Lord had made him over the years. And in perfect timing, not only did he want to see me at the first chance, no matter what part of the world I am, but The Lord Christ Jesus has caused him to believe in me and my brand so much, that he is willing to invest large sums of money in me. This, my friend, is the infinite, wondrous and divine power of the hand of The Lord!

More and more am I beginning to realize my gift from above. It was not long ago that I began to write and think of Benjamin for the first time in such a long time. And now, Benjamin has appeared out of the clear blue, into my world again.

Chapter 14

Also, I wasn't going to include my next recent testimony, however my spirit won't allow me to continue in my writing to you without sharing what was without a doubt, one of the single most joyous and happiest days of my life! It is an honor to share it with you.

About four months ago, as I was writing about my first grade teacher, Mrs. Hailey, I decided to search for her on Facebook. To my disappointment she was not registered on Facebook. I was quite sad.

Then, about a month afterwards, for some reason, I decided to go ahead and try searching for her name on Facebook again. And behold, Mrs. Hailey, who, just a month before, was nowhere to be found, had just opened a Facebook account. I could not believe my eyes. I gave thanks to Christ! I was extremely ecstatic!

"Is that you Mrs. Hailey?" I eagerly asked as I sent her a friend request. A short while later, I received a message from her.

"Boy, have you grown up! How are you and your family?"

She actually remembered me. I was so happy! I immediately replied. "Wow! I'm glad I found you on FB Mrs. Hailey! I can't believe you remember me :-) My family and I are doing well... You were the best 1st grade teacher! :-) I miss u! I'll have to stop by and visit soon... Thanks so much for giving me a head start!"

Then, Mrs. Hailey replied: "I am so happy that you are doing well! I would love to see you. Please let me know when it is a good time for you. I know you are very busy. I can't wait to tell my students about you. You certainly are a great role-model for them. I knew I would hear wonderful things about you one day. You were such a well mannered, bright young man. Please send my regards to your parents, brother and sister. :)"

Wow! That reply absolutely touched my heart from the second that I read it. It almost brought tears to my eyes. I could not believe that after 20 long years and hundreds of students later, she not only remembered me, but she also remembered that I had a sister and brother. My heart was truly touched in a way that it had never been touched before. With just that message, Mrs. Hailey made me feel more valued and special than I had ever felt before! It takes a very special teacher and human being to be able to remember details of a child's life after two decades. I was so touched, that I shared the divine story every chance that I got, with my close friends and family. I had planned on traveling to London that summer's end, so I told Mrs. Hailey that I would come and visit her and her new students upon my return at the beginning of the school year. My trip to London was postponed. My schedule got extremely busy. Month after month went by and I was unable to make the time to visit the school. But I always kept Mrs. Hailey and the children in my thoughts.

Then, after a few days into the week of November, when all was perfectly aligned, the spirit inside me pushed me to send Mrs. Hailey a message.

I said, "Hey Mrs. Hailey, sorry it took so long – I'd love to come visit you and speak to the kids towards the end of the month. Blessings until then! -Maubrey"

Then, two weeks later, I ecstatically sent and confirmed another message.

"How does Monday, Nov 23rd sound Mrs. Hailey? :-)"
She replied, "Great! I can't wait to see you!"

The wheels of joy were set in motion! For the following days leading up to Monday, November 23, 2009, I could not contain the joy and excitement that I felt inside! You could see the bright smile on my face everywhere I went. I told friends, strangers I had just met, anyone that I spoke to, that I was going to visit my first grade teacher after all these years. Everyone was just so happy and excited for me. This is the type of blessing that comes but a few times in life. I was well aware and grateful for the opportunity – the priceless gift that The Lord was blessing me with.

The Sunday night before, my excitement was peaking! I could barely sleep that night! It felt like the upcoming Monday morning was the first day of school. My chest was filled with great joy! I live in New Jersey, hours away from my old elementary school in Brooklyn, NY. So early in the morning, I awoke and gave thanks to The Lord Jesus for this momentous day. I shaved, showered, prepared and ate a big breakfast, and was on my way to visit my wonderful teacher and her students!

On the train route to Brooklyn, I stopped in Manhattan to buy the children some chocolate candy, and scoured the store for much time in search for the perfect and meaningful card to buy for Mrs. Hailey.

Next, I was on the train ride to my former elementary school, Public School 139(P.S. 139). I anxiously sat on the train, waiting for my stop, as I wrote a sincere and heartfelt note in the card to Mrs. Hailey. I recall a couple who noticed me writing in the card asking me if the card was for someone's birthday. You could not help, but to notice great happiness and the big bright smile on my face as I wrote the note.

"No." I answered, still with a cheerful smile on my face, "It's for my first grade teacher. I'm going to visit her for the first time in 20 years!"

The couple marveled at the thought, and were so happy for me.

Finally, it was my train stop! Cortelyou Road, Brooklyn, NY. Wow...! The second I stepped foot out of the train, it was like I had traveled back in time! Even now, my eyes water with tears, as I write about how spiritually wonderful I felt, as I remembered how, once, when I was young, I ran across the train tracks with some school friends. I took my precious time to soak in all that I was experiencing at that moment in time.

When I exited the train station and entered the street, I was aware that the school was just a few blocks away, to the left of the train station.

Perhaps, I was too much in a daze of nostalgic euphoria to see a school in the distance, so after walking a block, I asked a gentleman if he knew where the elementary school, P.S. 139 was.

"Oh, it's right there." he said nonchalantly, as he pointed to the school.

The moment I laid my eyes on the school, that is when it all hit me! I fought to hold back tears that were in my eyes. After 20 long years, I had come back! A wave of emotions flowed throughout my entire body. For the past few months leading to that moment, I had daydreamed of how the school looked. I wondered whether the image that had been imprinted in my mind when I was last at the school, almost two decades ago was how the school really looked like.

To my amazement, the school was exactly how I remembered it as a child. I was filled with so much happiness! I eagerly walked closer and closer to the school. When I got to the corner, I saw a group of women congregated there. I had a feeling that they were teachers, just taking a break for fresh air. I asked them whether they knew where the main entrance was. "Maubrey...!?" one of the women asked with a smile.

"Hi." I replied also with a smile. "Yes, I'm Maubrey."

Mrs. Hailey was so proud of me and excited to see me that she had told most of the teachers, the principal, and the students that I was coming that afternoon. I felt so humbled. The women introduced me to the principal, who happened to be walking into the school. Then I briefly conversed with her as she took me to see my first grade teacher. She knocked and slowly opened the door as I waited behind her.

"I have a guest for you Mrs. Hailey." the principal said with a big smile on her face.

It was one of the happiest moments of my life when I finally saw Mrs. Hailey. You could surely tell by the big smile on my face. We gave one another a great, long hug. I gave her the card that I bought for her and the chocolate for the children. To my pleasant surprise, she had a beautiful, gold, gift wrapped present for me as well. It was a very nice black leather wallet, custom made with my initials 'M.D.' engraved on it. Wow! I was so grateful for the unexpected surprise gift.

Next, she introduced me to the four year old, pre-kindergarten children, the most amazing children I've ever been privileged to be around.

"This is my student from a long time ago…" Mrs. Hailey said to the amazed and wide-eyed children.

I then spoke to the kids about eating healthy foods, working out, and staying active. I taught them how to do pushups and situps. It was truly the most adorable and heart melting thing to see them do pushups and situps for the first time in their lives. It was simply mind blowing for me to know that I was the first person to teach them how to work out for the first time. One discovers the simple wisdom he takes for granted. What an honor that was for me!

After I told the children that the way I first started becoming muscular was because I always loved to dance when I was their age, Mrs. Hailey put in a children's tape into the music player, and then the children, Mrs. Hailey and I all danced together for some time. I laugh now. I felt like I was on the set of a children's TV show. What an amazing experience! What a joy that was for me. I got to help serve them food in the class during their lunch time.

Then, Mrs. Hailey and I caught up on our lives, as she gave me a tour of my old elementary school. I remember being immediately taken back in time once again, the moment we entered the cafeteria. It had the same exact delicious aroma as it did 20 years ago! It put an even bigger smile on my face from the moment we walked inside.

Then, she took me to the playground and then to the auditorium, where she reminded me that I performed in a few school plays.

Next, she introduced me to some of the other teachers and faculty members in the school. It was such an honor and a privilege to meet them all. I could see the goodness in their faces. I could see the love in their hearts.

Finally, we returned to class and took many pictures together, as well as with all the children. But I'd have to say that what was probably one of the biggest highlights of my visit was when Mrs. Hailey gave me the opportunity to read two books to the children. 'Curious George' and 'The Gingerbread Man'... I cherished every precious moment while reading to the children, as they attentively hung on to every word that I read. I captured in my memory, every little detail of the experience, like the camera lights that flashed from Mrs. Hailey's digital camera, as I read to the children, and the brief wrestling battle that two adorable 3 or 4 year old boys were having right underneath my legs during the middle of my reading. I smiled inside my heart. They reminded me of two adorable lion cubs wrestling on the ground.

After I finished reading 'The Gingerbread Man' to them, Mrs. Hailey cleverly surprised the children with gingerbread cookies on behalf of me. The precious looks on their faces were priceless. They loved me even more.

All of a sudden, before I even realized how much time had gone by, I watched as Mrs. Hailey began to hand out coats and jackets to the children. At that moment, I realized that my wonderful experience was coming to a close. Where had time gone? My heart was touched further as the adorable children asked me to help them put their jackets on for them.

The kids always walked outside to the playground to meet their parents at the end of the day while holding hands with a partner. I remember my heart melting even more when one of three boys who wanted to hold my hand started crying because he didn't get to hold my hand all for himself. I comforted him telling him not to cry, and that they could all share my hands. "Are you coming back tomorrow Mr. Maubrey?" one adorable child asked me.

At that moment, I became so sad that I wouldn't be able to come. In just a few hours, the children had grown to love me. And I had fallen in love with them. It was truly an amazing feeling!

"I can't come tomorrow, but I'll definitely come back to visit you guys again."

I sincerely hope with all my heart that I can hold true to that promise.

When we got outside to the playground, all the children wanted to play the game tag with me before their parents arrived. The next thing you know, I was being chased by more than a dozen of the most adorable group of children that I have ever seen.

Minutes later, parents began to pick the children up. And with a blink of an eye, my absolutely wonderful and forever cherished day was over.

I took a few pictures and signed an autograph for an older, bright, young girl and her mom that Mrs. Hailey had told them about me. Then, I gave her some motivational words of encouragement, telling her that she could achieve all her dreams if she only believes.

Mrs. Hailey and I conversed as we walked to the corner of the block. We hugged, and parted ways, with the lasting memories that only Christ could have showered us with. What an unforgettable experience that truly was for me! What an unforgettable experience...

Chapter 15

Now, time travel back to the past with me, as I held the black phone handset, speaking to my best friends on the opposite end of a two inch thick, bulletproof glass window. After my best friends assured me that they would do all that they could to raise the funds to bail me out of jail, their visiting time was up. One after another, each of my dear friends said their final goodbyes, and encouraged me to stay positive in there. I was taken away from my friends and sent back to my cell block. It was a cold reminder of how much freedom and joy I had been deservingly deprived of.

I had been incarcerated for what seemed to be an infinite week now. I didn't know how much longer I could continue the same mundane routine of waking up at about 4am in the morning for breakfast, immediately going back to sleep on the floor in my corner underneath the stairs, then waking up again some hours later in the early morning for what was to be lunch.

I made attempts to remove myself from my current environment by continually drawing sketches, reading books, and working out. I never joined any groups or clicks in the jail. I never played cards with my fellow inmates. I simply kept reserved, unless someone came over to speak with me. As I had been from the moment that I entered the cell block, I had one focus – getting out!

About a week and a half later of me continually following up with Stella, I received the news that I had been diligently praying and believing for. Stella had successfully convinced my friends to bail me out with the majority of their money in their bank accounts. My angel had come through! But my blue skies quickly turned gray when later, she told me that they weren't able to find a bail bonds company that was willing to pay the $20,000 dollar bail to the court without substantial collateral like a car or house. None of my friends had an expensive car that they could put up as collateral, let alone, a home. In shock, my heart sank deeply in regards to the bad news.

Did God want to punish me in jail for much time because of the sins I had committed? I had to get myself back together. It was imperative that I stayed strong in there!

For the next few days, I scrambled through the phonebook directory, in search for a bail bonds company that would be willing to bail me out without collateral.

It's amazing – during those few days, after my prison mates found out that my friends had raised the money, I recall nearly the entire cell block population behind me, in support, doing anything they could do, and giving me valuable advice and encouragement.

Finally, a good man, who was also in jail for drug dealing, and had been incarcerated a few times before, suggested a number to a bail bonds woman who he had used in the past. I said a prayer, made the call, told her that her former client recommended her, and then explained my entire dilemma.

After some hesitation on her part, and my pleading and assurance that I would show up to all of my court dates, she agreed to put up the $20,000 dollar bail!

My spirit, at that very moment soared through the prison walls and into the sky! It was surely an unexplainable, unforgettable feeling. I immediately called Stella and told her the good news. I could almost see her weep with joy on the opposite end of the phone. She had been through so much – so many sleepless nights for me in the past days. The familiar intercom speaker with the voice of a prison officer sounded off with the names of inmates to be released that night.

A wave of emotions now rises throughout my entire body. I fight to hold back tears, and keep my hands from shaking, while writing in this populous public library, as I just now realized that, on this exact week, Saturday, December 5, 2009, exactly 7 years ago from this week, at last, I had heard my name being mentioned on the intercom that I was being released from jail!

"Mo...berr...ey Ok...Qua...sahh..." the officer on the intercom said, completely mispronouncing my name.

I did not care. Those words, out of the officer's mouth were like music to my ears!

Exactly 14 days after my arrest, by the Almighty Grace of God, I was freed! I was freed!! I was freed!! My diligent prayers had been answered! The Lord Jesus Christ had swooped down from Heaven and rescued me from heartache once again! It was truly a surreal feeling in that cell block at that moment. It seemed as if everyone in the cell block had frozen.

I vividly remember the deep, warm, emotional feeling in my chest after my name was called. The room stood quiet for a moment. All eyes were on me. Everyone in the cell block had been rooting for me. They all knew and proclaimed in days past, that I did not belong there.

One after another, inmate after inmate came up to me hugging me, shaking my hand, and congratulating me. It was a team effort to get me out. That type of love and camaraderie, my friend, is what the best morsels of life is all about! People like those... Experiences like that!

I may not remember most of their names, but I will always hold dear to my heart, how regally they treated me during my brief time with them. I still miss them all. They truly had a positive and lasting effect on my life.

It was now time for me to reunite with my best friends and face the outside world. I remember standing in the elevator with the prison officer as he transported me down to the main floor to retrieve the clothes that I had on, on the day of my arrest. With a bright smile on my face, and shaking my head, I told him, "You will never see me here again!" The officer smiled. But I think he knew how serious I was.

It took such a long time to get my clothes and sign numerous papers before I was allowed to go to the room where my friends, Stella, Gavin, Landon, Gabriel, and Nicholas waited anxiously to see me again.

My heart filled with much gladness from the moment that I entered the secluded room and saw their smiling faces. Together, we all hugged a warm hug for some time.

Then, it was my Stella and me. I looked deep into her bluish-green eyes and wrapped my arms around her. She wrapped her arms around my body. I could feel her heart beating through her layers of clothes. We stood there hugging for what seemed to be forever, fighting back a sea of tears. Our hearts seemed to have synced together. We were one. At that moment, our love for one another could have saved the world! It was that deep...that intense...that pure...that powerful!

I inhaled a deep breath of fresh air the moment I stepped outside into the night time streets. It was like no other feeling. At that moment, I had enough energy and happiness to run all the way home.

When my friends and I arrived at my apartment, that had been vacant for two weeks now, my apartment was completely trashed. Furniture was torn and upside down, the food in my fridge was spoiled, an entire bag of sugar was emptied into my kitchen sink, all my possessions were scattered on my bedroom floor, and my suitcase and dresser drawers were emptied out.

The first thing I did the moment that I entered the apartment was walk straight to my closet where I had my secret stash can safes, with the money and drugs in them. I was hoping that there was a chance that Stella had overlooked the safes. I could pay my friends the over $2000 dollars back that night and still have much money to last me for many months. My safes were gone! There was nothing but actual canned goods in my closet.

Then, I remembered that I had about a few ounces of psychedelic mushrooms left just before my arrest. I had different hiding places for different drugs in my apartment. I had hidden it in such an ambiguous place – just behind my study desk in my room, where you could clearly see the wall through the space where your legs belonged. Except, I had bought a white, 3'x3' foot cardboard paper that was the same color of the painting of the wall. I placed it behind the leg area of my study desk and simply put the bag of psychedelic mushrooms between the cardboard paper and the wall. If you stood in front of the desk and looked at the leg space, the wall colored cardboard created an illusion that you were looking at the room wall.

"They had to have found the mushrooms in their thorough sweeping of my apartment." I thought to myself.

But I was hopeful and optimistic that they didn't find it. I stretched my hand behind the desk as my friends looked on in anticipation. I navigated my hands from side to side. Then suddenly, I felt a plastic bag! My heart jumped. I smiled. My friends thought that I was joking. I pulled it up, from the back of the desk and held it in the air with excitement. My friends and I were in complete shock. We could not believe it! The bag of psychedelic mushrooms was still there. My heart raced with excitement, and then, immediately, my mind filled with fear and cautious paranoia. This feeling was too familiar. I had felt this same feeling in my chest before, just a few weeks ago, when Connor called asking to buy hundreds of ecstasy pills from me. So many thoughts flooded my mind. Should I sell it right away to my many customers, who had been ringing my phone off the hook for the weeks that I was in jail? Had I not learned my lesson from going to jail and losing all my freedom? Was this a trap, strategically left by the police to ensure that, this time, I would go to jail without the possibility of parole? Or was my hiding place so clever and brilliant, that the police didn't think of looking there?

I consulted with my friends. Stella, of course, was completely against it. The others did not advise of me selling it. They seemed a bit indifferent. After all, I was a 19 year old adult. I got the felling though, that they would not mind if I sold it, based on their reactions. I did, indeed owe them about $2,500 dollars.

This was a moment of truth. I had a big decision to make. I decided to keep it hidden until I figured out what to do. I spent the next couple of hours in my apartment with the best friends in the world that The Lord could possibly give a person. We talked. We laughed. They sat around me in awe as I told them the entire story of how it was from the moment Connor entered my apartment to buy the drugs, to the time the police officers knocked on my apartment door, to my first morning waking up on the floor in a jail cell block, to the food that I had to eat, to the many great characters that I lived with during those two long weeks, up until the emotional moment that I heard my name being called on the intercom.

Later, my friends hugged me and welcomed me back home, then went to their apartments just across the pond. Stella stayed behind. My angel. That night, we made passionate, sweet love to the sound of music playing in the crystal clear December air.

The following morning, just like me, I was back to business. I had a lot to do. I had a lot of decisions about which direction my life would go. I was now a drug dealer on parole, facing up to 60 years in prison. Not my mother, not my father, not any of my family or any of my friends could deliver me out of this circumstance that I had placed myself in. I knew that the only one that could save me was God...El Shaddai...The Almighty...Jesus Christ!

The first thing that I had to do was to clean and organize my apartment back to a spotless haven. Then, I had to decide whether to throw away the ounces of psychedelic mushrooms, or sell them.

What did I decide? Foolishly, I decided to do what any desperate, 19 year old, drug dealer would do. I decided that I was going to sell it! But who could I trust? Who could I sell it to? I pondered long about it. I combed through my contact list, eliminating client after client.

Then finally, I came unto a name of a girl, who I knew I could trust, who was completely anti-law enforcement. Despite, you never know how things, and people's views on topics could change within a blink of an eye. I had made the decision! I was going to take a chance!

Fortunately, my instincts served me right. She came to my apartment, bought the psychedelic mushrooms, and for the first time in about a year, I was finally rid of all illegal drugs from my home! I was free from the drug dealing lifestyle. I now had a limited amount of money. I would only be able to survive in Bloomington on my own for another month or two. And there wasn't a single thought in my mind that told me to get a normal 9 to 5 job. I was a thinker. I was an entrepreneur. I was a leader. I was an innovator. I knew that I had to dig deep into the depths of my mind to figure out how I could legally become prosperous and wealthy.

Chapter 16

EUREKA MOMENT

I spent the following days in solitude, taking long walks through town, meditating in my apartment, pondering what I could possibly do to thrive. Then, I started searching the internet for money making ideas. Soon, I was going online all day, every day, looking for wholesale products to buy and resell for huge profits. For me, the wholesale route was the obvious choice, since I had been so good at it, while dealing drugs. The wholesale opportunities on the internet were decent, but they were nowhere near the profit margins that I was earning as a drug dealer.

Meanwhile, all my former drug customers continued to call me in search of drugs. Sometimes, I told them that I was out of the drug game. Sometimes, I referred another dealer to them. Sometimes, I simply didn't answer my phone. You begin to realize that the moment you retire from doing what you love and are really great at doing, people tend to value you, and your services substantially more. And I was great at what I did! And I loved every exciting moment of it!

Soon, the requests for my drug dealing services greatly multiplied. I knew that I was missing out on a lot of money. I thought of a few ways of making drug related money without being directly in contact with the drugs. At first, I tried getting a percentage of the profits from other dealers, for any customer that I recommended to them. Then, I called a handful of other drug dealers that I knew, and offered to give them all my customers for over $10,000 dollars.

Needless to say, neither idea was successful. I thought hard for many days for an answer to my financial problems, and then one day, my eureka moment came!

I recall being in my apartment complex's computer lab, when I decided to search for legal herbal ecstasy. I wanted to fill the demand of my old clients, but not risk going to jail at the same time. I had found the perfect solution, I thought. I spent days, and countless hours researching the internet, doing my due diligence, and reading testimonial after testimonial of the ecstasy-like effects of different types of legal ecstasy. And there were over a dozen types to choose from.

Finally, after much research, with about $100 dollars left in my bank account, I decided to order a sample of two or three different herbs that had the most testimonials of creating ecstasy-like effects. I took a gamble! Consequently, the gamble paid off. About a week after receiving the sample pills in the mail, I was sold out! I told no one that they were legal herbal pills. I lied and said that the pills, and powder, in some cases, were different types of ecstasy. I knew it was wrong, but I was more concerned about making money again. Each time I sold out, I used the proceeds to buy more and more quantity. I was back in business!

Next, I decided to start an online business. Plus, I knew that I had to have a legitimate stream of income. I remember spending hundreds of hours, day and night, developing a wholesale website from scratch. I taught myself the computer language, html. I constantly paid for money making opportunities advertised on the internet. I was determined and eager to become a success.

Soon, I asked my friends to drive me, miles away to apply for my first business license. I was doing it! I was making it happen! Despite the fact that I was facing 60 years in jail, if convicted, I was surely beginning to move forward again. Between the money coming in from selling wholesale products online, and selling the herbal pills to a select number of customers, I was surviving again. I had nowhere as near the number of clients as I did when I was selling authentic illegal drugs, but it would have to do for the time being. I was content to be able to eat and pay my bills.

Sales-wise, some weeks were good, and some weeks were great weeks. I recall throwing lavish grey goose and belvedere vodka parties again. I even made huge signs of my company's name, and posted them on my apartment walls during the parties, as a form of advertising and marketing my new company.

From the very beginning of my release from jail, I remained eternally positive, and fearless, that The Lord would deliver me from going to jail for 60 years. You would never be able to tell, by the constant cheer in my face, by the daily celebrations of life, that I was a man that could possibly be going to jail for the rest of my life. My attitude exuded with confidence.

Things were going smoothly in my life, but then, I soon discovered one consequence of being arrested and having a judge ordered search warrant for my apartment. I received a notice of eviction from the management office of my apartment complex. When you get arrested for dealing illegal drugs out of an apartment complex, whether you are found guilty or not, the police must notify the management office. In turn, the management office has the right to evict you (I'm sure our mustard and ketchup carpet incident didn't help).

Within a few months of my eviction notice, I was out in the cold and in the snow, with all my possessions. Against the apartment management's wishes, I moved into my friends, Gabriel, Gavin, and Landon's apartment. The management were, to say the least, not fond of me being in the complex. I fully understood. Why would any management want a suspected drug dealer on the premises?

Days after my eviction date, they kept seeing me on the complex during various hours of the day. They must have surely realized that I wasn't just visiting my friends. Soon, the management began to send maintenance workers to my friends' apartment where I was staying to confirm that I was indeed living in the vacant bedroom of my three friends' four bedroom apartment. Their suspicion was confirmed. Next, they threatened to evict my friends if anyone, meaning me, was caught in the vacant bedroom again.

I was desperate. I had nowhere to go. My friends agreed to allow me to sleep in the living room. Before long, my friends received a letter from the apartment management office warning that they could face eviction again, if a guest stayed in their apartment longer than a few days. The management office was determined to drive me out of the complex. My friends, however, stuck up for me at first. They let me sleep hidden, on the floor in a small space between a sofa and the wall.

However, after many days of constant eviction threats, I had to move out. There was no getting around this. My friends suggested that I go back home, not necessarily because I was inconveniencing them, but more out of concern for my well-being. Looking back, it is amazing to think about the immovable state of mind that I was in at such an early age. Still, the thought of leaving the paradise that I had created for myself in Bloomington, Indiana was nowhere in my mind. I would do everything in my divine power to stay!

Another close friend, Daniel, who eventually ended up being another of my dearest and cherished lifetime friends, suddenly had a vacant room in his apartment. I've been blessed to be able to form the strongest bonds with people, simply by living with them for a few months, and even a few weeks. I am eternally grateful to all my companions who have helped me at my greatest times of need. It was a true blessing from above. Daniel gladly agreed that, if I could contribute in any way, then I could live in the second bedroom of his apartment, until I was able to get back on my feet.

Chapter 17

My new roommate, Daniel, and I got along just fine. I tried my best to be a good roommate to him. From day one, I got right to work in building my online business. I knew that it was a long road ahead for me if I wanted to be successful. Daniel, for obvious reasons, didn't want me to sell what he and everyone else thought were ecstasy pills in his apartment. So, my income decreased dramatically. I wasn't too worried though. I would now have more time to focus on my business. I remember being on the computer all day, and all hours of the night tirelessly designing my website, searching for and networking with potential suppliers and customers.

Some nights, I would sit in front of the computer for so long, that for the first time in my life, I would have hallucinations due to sleep deprivation. On many occasions, I would stay in the apartment for days at a time without even noticing it. There was nothing for me outside the apartment. The only times that I would go out was to parties, during the weekends.

Other times, I'd be in front of the computer, then suddenly, the sun would rise early in the morning. I became engulfed with my work. This was my newest love! There were a few times in the beginning, that I mismanaged and lost a few customers' money. Consequently, I was reported to the Bloomington Police Department by a customer from another part of the country. Under normal circumstances, I believe, the report would have been taken lightly by the police. However, I was a prime target for the law. This was their opportunity to re-arrest me and force me to give them the name of my supplier. Since I originally started the business in my friends' Gabriel, Landon, and Gavin's apartment, back at the University Commons, the business address was registered as their apartment address.

So, around early to mid March, while the boys were away on spring break vacation, and five months after my arrest, the Bloomington Police paid a visit to their apartment. They had no idea that I had just moved out just a short while before. The police found nothing in my best friend's apartment but a few grams of marijuana that was in Landon's room. My mind was blown, when Landon told me that during his interrogation by the police upon his return from vacation, all that the detectives kept telling him was, "We just want Maubrey...!" I was enlightened to realize the determination of the police to re-arrest me. It certainly put my circumstance into perspective.

Then, there was another time shortly after, that I was almost re-arrested again. It was surely one of the most heart-racing moments in my life up to that point. I had been drinking at the apartment of some Indiana University football player friends of mine, when we all decided to go out to the nightclub around 2am in the morning. We were standing there in front of the nightclub hanging out, when out of nowhere, a police officer appeared from the dark alley on the side of the club. I remember it as if it were yesterday. There were about five of us outside that nightclub. The police officer could definitely tell, by our body language, that we had been drinking. The officer called us to question us. My heart raced! If I was arrested for underage drinking, there was a great possibility that I would not see day light until after my drug case was completed. I had to think fast and make a split decision.

With a blink of an eye, I was off to the races! My mind went blank. I had never run that fast, with that much adrenaline pumping in my body in my life! At that point, there was no turning back. I was running away from a police officer. I don't remember, however the officer must have given up chase after a few strides. The football players joked and teased me the following day, that they had never seen anyone run that fast in their lives. In my sandals and shorts, I dashed down the first corner to my left, sprinting down the street. Midway to the corner of that block, during my frantic escape, I heard the screaming siren of a police car. I panicked! As I made a quick right at the end of the block into the one-way, busy street that night, I saw the police car racing toward my direction. I switched gears and maximized my speed! I remember noticing some sort of large sign on the sidewalk. As the police car raced toward my direction, I pumped my legs and hands as fast as I could to use the sign as a shield between the speeding police car and me. Just a millisecond slower, and the officer would have seen a sprinting man darting in his direction.

Or perhaps, the officer saw me and could not come to an abrupt halt in the middle of a one way street. The police car was now behind me, speeding in the opposite direction. With my heart pounding and full of fright, I darted into the local waffle house restaurant. Completely out of breath and exhausted, I quickly ducked down in that doorway area of the waffle house for at least an hour, calling Daniel and Stella, and leaving them hysterical messages that I may be finally going to jail once more. Reality really hit me that night. I had to be very careful with the actions that I made from then on! After over an hour, when it seemed safe to go outside, I journeyed a long, quiet, reflective walk back home. The next day, after the scare, I was back to business.

Chapter 18

My journey moved forward. It was now late spring of 2003. School had ended for all the students in Indiana University. The United States had officially entered into war with Iraq. The price of pure gold was only about $350 dollars per ounce.

Only now, as I reflect, do I realize that I was surrounded by much counterfeit forces. In addition to the counterfeit ecstasy pills that I was selling, I began to sell counterfeit accessories and apparel and cubic zirconium diamond jewelry. I did not lie about the authenticity of the jewelry, as they were obviously not authentic, however, with my state-of-mind during those days, I wonder if I would have lied if I could get away with it. I probably would have.

There was a time that I ran into an old jail mate in a nightclub. When I sold him the counterfeit pills, I realized after he had left, that he had paid me with counterfeit currency. I was upset and offended, but how could I blame him? After all, that was what I was attracting into my life.

I began selling the cubic zirconium diamond jewelry and counterfeit accessories and apparel on consignment to all the local urban stores in town. This was yet another idea to increase my cash flow. I even began sitting in a barber shop all day selling my products as I studied my biology pre-med book, still determined to somehow return to school the following semester. I was simply determined not to fail. As a result of my persistence and hard work, my finances began to improve again.

Then one fateful evening at a nightclub on the weekend, there he was! Connor! The man who was responsible for putting me in jail. The man who I once trusted. The man who betrayed me. With the look on my face that I gave him, he must have known that I had no good thoughts for him. Still, he approached me. He told me that he heard that I was arrested and that the police had arrested him that day as well. I may never find out for sure, but based on my instincts and the detailed police report that I was given, I knew that he was lying. I immediately became on high alert. I suspected what was going on. The Bloomington Police must have strategically planted him there to get a confession or any violent reaction out of me. I was too wise for that.

It is strange. That night, I experienced mixed emotions. Part of me wanted to attack him for betraying me. However, another part of me wanted to give him a big hug for forever changing my life, and preventing me from going down a dangerous and deadly path that I was not prepared for. At that moment, he was an enemy and an angel to me. I removed myself from his presence for the remainder of the night.

As if the night wasn't strange and random enough, later, in front of the nightclub, after it had closed, a guy around my age, who had a striking resemblance to Connor, with a similar height, lanky body size, and pale faced look as Connor, approached me, asking me whether I had any drugs to buy. As I had always done in the past with illegal drugs, I had some herbal ecstasy on my person. Suspiciously and cautiously, I engaged in conversation with him. I remember him asking me if I wanted to go to Joseph Diggs house, directly adjacent to the club.

"Who's Joseph Diggs?" I asked.

"He's the actor, Taye Digg's brother." he replied.

I agreed to go. I figured that it would be safe since it was the brother of a celebrity's house. I sold the guy the herbals, and then went to the door of Joseph Diggs. The guy, whose name escapes me, introduced me to Joseph. "This is Mike.", the guy said, referring to me, since most of the students at Indiana University called me by my middle name, Mike.

"Hey…" replied Joseph Diggs.

He invited the guy and me into his home, which was directly next to the nightclub. I had no idea that this was going to be a divine connection between Joseph and me. We spent a few hours at Joseph's apartment, late, that night. There were already a handful of people at his home when we arrived. We spent the majority of the time having a few drinks, listening to music and talking.

I will never forget the story that Joseph Diggs told the group that night. The short story truly changed my life and had a major impact in the coming decision that I was to make. Joseph told about how he was arrested for a drug charge years ago. He spoke about how the police kept trying to offer him a deal to plead guilty to prevent him from going to prison for an extended time. Time after time, Joseph said he refused to plead guilty or betray any drug dealer. He said that he was sure that the police did not have enough evidence to prove him guilty. He testified to us that finally, after about two long and trying years, the case against him was miraculously, completely dropped!

That single story completely blew my mind. It was exactly what I needed to hear. I knew that The Lord had placed me in that specific moment and location to hear that story. That testimony was meant for me. There Joseph was, telling this personal and emotional story to virtually complete strangers, having absolutely no idea that I had been arrested, and was out on parole, facing 60 years in prison if convicted. Joseph had no idea what hearing that story meant for me. The story gave me a renewed sense of hope and optimistic confidence for my future. Only about five months after my arrest, Christ had given me a divine foresight into what battles were coming ahead. I would use this divine story to hold ground and press forward throughout my tribulations.

The very next day, the guy that I had met in front of the nightclub and sold the herbals to, called me, wanting to come to my apartment to buy some more. I recall him attempting to ask a few questions and extend our phone conversation. I immediately interrupted, telling him to just come by and "hang out". I had been through this telephone routine countless times with new and long-term clients who wanted to have conversations on the phone. I had become highly efficient, especially after my arrest, in cutting the conversations extremely short.

Could I trust this guy, who eerily, reminded me of Connor, the man who betrayed my trust? Once again, I went with my instincts. Although I was a bit nervous, as I always was with every transaction, especially with a new client, I was not too worried. I knew that I had taken all my usual precautions. And I figured that at the worst case scenario, if arrested, at least the pills and powder that I was selling wasn't illegal drugs.

When I got off the phone with him, my buddy, Aiden, who was on the Indiana University football team, called me, telling me that he was in the area and was going to stop by the apartment for a bit.

"Sure." I said. "Come on over..."

A few minutes later, Aiden was in my apartment. It was always good to see my friend Aiden. He was a huge, 6'5" 270 plus pound, defensive tackle. I had not known him long before that afternoon. However, he knew that I was a wrestler, and I knew that he was a football player. We had seen each other out at nightclubs and on campus numerous times throughout the previous two school years. I recall him always being positive and full of energy and excitement whenever he saw me. I certainly appreciated that.

So, while I waited for my new customer to show up at my apartment, Aiden and I hung out in the living room telling jokes, talking about women, talking about our plans to go to the nightclub that evening, and shared stories of the fun and exciting highlights of the previous school year.

Suddenly, I heard a knock on the door. It was my new customer. I invited him into the apartment, told Aiden that I would be with him in just a short while, and then sold two or three pills to the guy in my room. We shook hands and he left my apartment.

Aiden and I carried on in our conversation, storytelling and jokes. We had no idea what awaited us in the coming minutes. As we joked and laughed, both of our hearts were suddenly shocked with great fright.

Boom...! Like the tremendous sound of powerful thunder and lightning striking down a colossal tree in a peaceful secluded forest. Boom...! Boom...!

"Bloomington Police! Bloomington Police! Open up!"

Boom! Boom!

"Bloomington Police! Open Up...!"

I don't think I had ever before, been startled and surprised like that in my life! Aiden and I could see the old brown wooden apartment door being destroyed, as a huge hole in the middle of it was being created by the pounding force of the police officers. As if it were in slow motion, we watched wooden splinters of the door sailing across the living room. We watched in panic, as the hole in the door got bigger and bigger as a swat team of 200 plus pound, body builder sized, Bloomington Police Officers took turns using a heavy, black, metal, battling ram, and the power of their legs and feet, covered with heavy duty, reinforced, steel toe boots, to break through the old, brown, frail, wooden door.

In retrospect, it is a bit amusing, given how long it took the swat team to break through the door to get into the apartment that my friend and I were in. The door wasn't one of those solid, heavy-duty, wooden doors that you find in some homes. It was one of those cheaply made doors with just 3 or 4 pieces of thin wood used as an interior frame, and probably glued to 2 extremely thin, brown, wooden sheets, not more than a few millimeters thick. You could easily punch the door with your fist and make a hole in the door. But I guess the pattern that the door was shattering and splintering to pieces made it difficult for the swat team to break into the apartment faster.

I'll never forget the priceless look on Aiden's face when we heard the first bang on the door. We went from cracking jokes and laughing to quickly becoming wide eyed with extreme shock and surprise. We were frozen as we looked directly at each other's eyes in panic. I could almost tell you each mega pixel, every detail of Aiden's eyes. Aiden was like a deer caught in headlights at night, like a clip you would see in a movie, when the camera man quickly zooms into nothing but the actor's eyes. That's the look I saw on Aiden's face.

Time had frozen for us. Everything seemed to be happening in slow motion as the cops were yelling, "Open up! Bloomington Police! Open Up..!"

This time around, instead of my life flashing before my eyes, I saw my entire future flash before my eyes. It was surreal. This, like many previous situations in my life, felt like I was in a movie. Aiden and I could do nothing but watch in panic and shock, as the hole in the old, frail, wooden door grew larger and larger. If we wanted to get rid of any evidence, or shimmy down the third floor patio, we could have definitely done so in that entire minute or so, which to us, felt like an eternity. However, we could not move! We were absolutely frozen!

Every once in a while, before that day, I would imagine that if armed robbers, or cops ever tried to break into my apartment, as was currently happening, I would jump out of our third floor apartment patio, either onto the parking lot pavement, or preferably, onto a student's parked car to cushion my fall. I knew that either way, it would hurt badly, possibly breaking or fracturing bones in my body. But, I mentally prepped myself and tried to convince myself that I could do it if and when the time ever came.

"It wouldn't be that bad of a jump." I would say to myself. "I'm an athlete. I've jumped at least half this height with no problem or injuries before."

As a backup plan, I would imagine climbing over the balcony barrier, scaling down to the neighbors' balcony beneath ours, and either repeating the same steps all the way down to the first floor balcony. Or, after I had originally gotten to the first balcony directly below my balcony, I would rush into the neighbors' apartment below, and quickly escape through their door. I must have thought that I was a stuntman to even have had those wild ideas in my head. But I knew that it was always good to be prepared and have a plan, than to not have a plan at all. It would have had taken a bit more time and finesse to get to the neighbors' balcony and apartment below us, but I imagine, it would have been a lot better than laying on the parking lot pavement with a broken leg...right?

One of the officers had finally decided to kick the doorknob area to break the barrier and get into the apartment. One by one, with fire in their eyes, and stone cold looks on their faces, they came storming in like a gang of soldiers, guns drawn and pointed directly at Aiden and me.

They were yelling at the top of their voices, "Bloomington Police!! Freeze…! Freeze…! Hands up! Get down on the ground!! Get down on the ground!!"

I can assure you, they did not have to worry about the "freeze" part. We had that down pack!

We had gone from joking, laughing, and planning how fun the night out at the club was going to be, to now, suddenly surrounded by about ten to fifteen adrenalin raged Bloomington Police, Swat Team Officers.

It's a dizzying experience to look down a barrel of a gun and to see ten to fifteen steel handguns all pointed at you. The slightest wrong movement by either Aiden or me could have literally set off a violent round of gunshots that would have immediately ended both of our lives. We both knew it. We weren't going to take any chances.

Almost in sync, Aiden and I, Aiden still with the deer in headlights look in his eyes, (I imagine he saw me with the same deer in headlights look on my face) slowly put both our hands in the air, got on our knees, our backs turned away from the swat team, and faced the now irrelevant and useless sliding glass door and balcony that I had prepped to escape from. Still synchronized, we placed our sweaty palms on the old, dingy, light brown carpet. We lowered our chests to the carpet, then gently rested the sides of our faces on the carpet.

"Oh boy… Here we go again!" I thought to myself.

"BUSTED!"

Chapter 19

I was busted again! Poor Aiden. He had no idea, when he woke up that morning, that he would be in the middle of a major drug raid, and have multiple guns pointed at him. I felt terrible that he was caught in the middle of this situation.

I realized exactly what had happened. The guy who had just bought the herbal pills from me was a confidential police informant. I realized that everything had been planned from the time he approached me for drugs outside of the nightclub. I had been set up. Was I now going to spend the rest of my life in jail?

The police handcuffed Aiden and me, took Aiden to a bedroom to interrogate him, and interrogated me in the living room. With the intimidating size of Aiden, the police surely must have thought that he was my body guard.

Seconds after I was seated for interrogation, there he came walking in, almost in slow motion, like a scene in a movie that I had watched in the past. It was like a ghost in a trench coat; the detective, who had arrested me over a half a year ago. I thought I was looking at a ghost. It blew my mind to know and realize that I had been closely watched and followed all that time!

With a cynical look on his face, he said, "You are going to jail for a long time!"

I calmly replied immediately, "Can you tell me why I'm being arrested?"

He said that I had just sold some ecstasy pills to a confidential informant. So, I calmly asked them to show me the pills. They couldn't. It seems that the informant had ingested the pills that I sold him. I did recall him taking one or two before he left my apartment.

"That's odd..." I thought.

They were attempting to arrest me, however the informant had swallowed the evidence. The Lord was working in mysterious ways on my behalf yet again.

It was obvious to everyone in the apartment that I had just sold the informant pills, but I never admitted to the sale, even though I knew the pills were not illegal. I had learned a lot about how to behave when arrested after my first drug arrest. I was however, completely open with them that I had herbal pills in my possession. With all the reading and research that I had been doing, I had knowledge that there were no laws against having legal herbal hallucinogenic substances.

Meanwhile, the police interrogated Aiden in the other room, and thoroughly searched the apartment. At the time, herbal hallucinogens were completely unheard of by the general population, including the Bloomington Police Department. I was responsible for single handedly introducing and marketing a new product to the state of Indiana.

The detective, now with a baffled look on his face, refused to believe that the effects of the pills and powders that I was selling to the population came from a legal substance. I watched and listened, as the police ransacked the apartment.

"The pills are legal." I announced. "I'll even show you where I've hidden them."

To deter them from finding my main hiding place with the majority of the pills, I showed them one hiding place that I had kept just a few hundred pills. I had thousands and thousands of more pills hidden throughout the apartment! Bewildered, they examined the pills that I showed them.

"Real or not," the detective said, "Why are you selling fake ecstasy pills?"

I knew that this was an attempt to get me to admit to dealing.

Politely, I replied, "I'd like to cooperate officer, but I have no idea what you are talking about."

Next, I saw Aiden walking out of the room, unhandcuffed and quietly leaving my apartment. They realized that he was simply at the wrong place at the wrong time. Would they let me go as well? I wondered. No. I was on my way back to the police station, the one place that I promised myself that I would never go again! It felt as if my heart sank to the floor. Still, they could not believe that the pills were legal.

I was put in a cold, small, secluded room at the police precinct. I was handcuffed to the bench and left in the room alone for almost an hour while they searched online and chemically tested the pills to verify my story.

That night, alone in that cold room, handcuffed to the bench, I got down on the floor, and prayed a powerful prayer to The Lord to deliver me out of this circumstance; out of this bondage. I prayed that Christ enter the hearts of the detectives, and give them the desire to release me. Lying on that cold floor, I prayed and prayed to Jesus. I had goose bumps on my entire body. After much prayer, I dozed off to sleep on the floor. It was now around midnight. It had been a long exhausting day for me.

Suddenly, as I was falling into a deep sleep, I was awakened by a detective at the door. I had no idea what would happen next, but I was prepared. I was at peace with Christ. The detective uncuffed me and took me to another room to further interrogate me. It was just him and me in a small room. I sat across a desk from him. I observed a surveillance camera on the top corner of the wall pointed directly at us. The detective pulled out a pen and notepad, and then proceeded to interrogate me. After the first few questions, I was sure that my prayers had been answered! I knew that they did not have any evidence to arrest me, and that they had confirmed online, that the pills were legal. I became much more at ease. They had wasted so much time, resources, energy and money setting up and raiding my apartment. All for naught. Now, what they were hoping, was for me to think that I would be sent to jail if I did not work for them as a confidential informant.

The detective asked me many questions, attempting to get me to say as much as possible, in addition to attempting to get me to confess to my initial drug charges. I was far prepared for and aware of his interrogation tactics. They did not work. After much time of repeating that I knew nothing, and would be willing to fully cooperate once my attorney was present, the detective eventually realized his attempts to confuse and scare me were futile.

Finally, he asked, "So you mean to tell me that you don't know any drug dealers in town?"

I'll never forget my reply.

I looked him straight in the eye and answered, "Officer. This is a college town. There are about 30,000 students on campus. Everyone is a drug dealer in some way! I could go outside right now and point at anyone in the street, and I'd be sure that they do drugs or have sold drugs in one way or another before."

He was silenced.

Moments later, he asked me if I was sure that I wouldn't give up a name of a dealer, believing that I would think that if I didn't, then I would be taken to jail. Knowing that he was playing mind games with me, I decided to play mind games with him as well. I took a nickel out of my pocket, stood it upright on the table, and then spun it, giving him the impression that, whether the coin landed on heads or tails, would determine whether or not I would give him a drug dealer's name. There was no way, however, that I would cooperate, no matter which side of the coin that faced up when it stopped spinning. I had my morals about betraying another dealer. Plus, I knew that I had absolute leverage.

We both watched, as the coin spun. I stopped it with my right palm, slowly lifted my hand, took a deep breath, looked at the detective's face, and then told him that unfortunately, I could not help him. It was my one moment of amusement throughout that entire ordeal. The detective shook his head in obvious frustration, stood up, opened the door and left me in the interrogation room alone for quite some time.

Finally, the miraculous happened! The detective opened the door.

"You're free to go." he said, obviously annoyed.

My heart rejoiced with extreme happiness! Words could not express how I felt that night. I was truly humbled by the entire experience. Just like that, I could have been taken away from my friends, and sent to jail for a very very long time. I had escaped capture...for now. I had taught the Bloomington Police Department a very valuable lesson. As the interrogator let me out of the door, I looked him straight in the eye, and gave him the most sincere thank you. I was aware of what they had done for me. By the grace of God, they had really saved me! They could have easily decided to hold me in jail, despite all the evidence that I had provided them that the pills were not illegal.

I had no car or money to get back home. That night, with my brown sandals, khaki shorts, and brown, button down, short sleeve, collared shirt, I walked about a mile directly to the nightclub that Aiden and I had originally planned on going. It's interesting, the doorman usually gave me a hard time getting in because I was underage. But that night, my relief and excitement must have shined through my face. For the first time in countless times that I had been going there, he just let me in with absolutely no questions and no resistance. By the look on my face, anyone could tell that I had just experienced a wonderful life-changing miracle.

Aiden, when he saw me in the nightclub, just a few hours after the both of us were in the middle of an all-out, gun drawn drug raid, could not believe his eyes. He looked at me as if he was looking at a ghost that had come back from the dead. In reality, I did come back from a seemingly dead circumstance. That night, I celebrated like I had never celebrated before! At that moment, all my cares and concerns were washed away.

The following morning, once again, I had to move forward in my journey. I returned to the apartment. The shattered wooden door had been replaced by the maintenance staff. As I expected, a few days later, I was ordered by the management to vacate the apartment.

Chapter 20

I moved in with Aiden for a few weeks, then another friend for a few more weeks. When that friend's lease expired during the summer, I moved into another friend's apartment for about one month.

After that, I finally found an apartment to sublease for the summer. I was being forced to relocate constantly. The story of my life... I had become a burden to a lot of my friends. By the summer of that single year, I had moved and lived in a total of seven different apartments. From my beautiful apartment in the University Commons to my best friends' apartment across the pond. Then, to Daniel's apartment. Then Aiden's apartment, two other friends' apartments, then finally, the subleased one bedroom apartment. I was really learning to survive. If I thought that I was moved around a lot as a child, then that, in no way, compared to the amount of relocations that I was making in Bloomington.

Business slowed drastically from all the moving that I did that summer. But now, I finally had a place of my own – for the time being. I could sell the herbal ecstasy with no interference or distractions. I sold as many as I could to whoever was interested, but it was summertime, and most of the students were away. In addition, I was getting more and more complaints about the pills and powder, that they weren't real ecstasy. Every time, I lied and sometimes convinced my customers that they were genuine ecstasy. Some customers complained that they could not feel the effects. And then I increased the amount of powder that I filled each capsule with. Then customers complained that the pills were far too strong.

Soon, I was taking my own herbals once or twice a week, in attempt to achieve the perfect euphoric effect. That summer, I must have experimented over 20 times. Many wild nights resulted from taking those pills. That summer was filled with much herbals and alcohol consumption.

There was the usual crowd of us outside the nightclubs after a night of drinking. Fairly intoxicated, with a couple of Bloomington Police Officers standing just a few feet away, I recall foolishly telling a guy that I had never seen before, that I bet him that I would slap his burger down to the ground. Insulted, he warned me not to do it. I don't know what got into me that night, but seconds later, I slapped the guy's burger on the floor. I did it as a joke, knowing that I would pay for another burger for him. Obviously, he did not find it funny. He became highly aggressive and confrontational.

"Why did you knock my food down!?" he shouted.

His eyes raged. Just a few feet away from the on looking officers, he started to shove me.

"I'll buy you another one... I'll buy you another one..." I repeated quietly, while holding his arms down.

The last thing that I wanted to do was attract attention from the police. He only got louder and louder.

"Why did you knock my food down!?" he shouted again.

"What have I gotten myself into?" I thought to myself.

Seconds later, in front of everyone, both he and I were handcuffed and arrested for underage drinking. I could not believe what was happening. The Lord had just released me just weeks before. I was given a second life. And now I had jeopardized my freedom for such a foolish action.

"This is it!" I thought. "My chances have run out!"

I saw myself sitting in prison for at least a year, until my case went to trial. I saw my leverage of having the luxury of being out on bail while awaiting trial disappear into thin air. I was devastated, as I sat handcuffed in the ever familiar backseat of the police car.

I was transported to the precinct and held until morning in a small room with a handful of other drunkards, including the guy that I had slapped his food to the floor. I recall apologizing to him. He accepted my apology and also apologized for overreacting. It's amazing how The Lord orchestrates connections out of adversaries and adversities. We were able to have a brotherly bond that night, talk about our cases that we were both facing, and encourage one another that things would turn for the best.

By the grace of God, when morning came, I was told that I could be released as long as someone could pay a few hundred dollars to bail me out. I was enormously relieved! My Father, Christ had showed up once again, for His foolish son. He had used His supernatural keys to unlock the doors to my cell. Once more, my faith grew stronger.

I lived in that isolated, practically empty, one bedroom apartment, sleeping on the floor each day, eating canned foods, and dealing the pills to the limited number of clients left in Bloomington that summer.

Before long, my sublease had expired, and once again, I found myself outside the apartment, with all my possessions out on the lawn. Irresponsibly, I had made no prior arrangements as to where I would go. By then, I had become well accustomed to going with the flow. That hot, summer afternoon, I scrambled to call about a dozen friends in my phone. Most could not help me, especially on such short notice.

Chapter 21

      Finally, an older gentleman, in his late 30s to mid 40s, who I had recently been introduced to agreed to allow me to stay at his townhouse for some time, until I was able to get settled. The man was truly a lifesaver! I don't know what I would have done, or where I would have gone, if it weren't for him.

      I must say, it was certainly interesting living with him. It became clear that he loved and had affection for me. I'm not sure whether he was gay or not, but he certainly had a fetish for feet – African American men's feet in particular. Up until that point, my young 19 year old mind had never known that such fetishes existed. It was quite strange a notion to me.

From the beginning, I was upfront and honest with him, and I let him know my position that I was not gay or interested. He made unsuccessful attempts to convince me a few times, however, in general, for the few weeks that I lived with him, he respected my views, and never wanted to make me feel uncomfortable.

Integrity: Steadfast adherence to a strict moral or ethical code...the state of being unimpaired; soundness...the quality or condition of being whole or undivided; completeness.

"I have to commend you, Maubrey." I recall him telling me a number of occasions. "You certainly have integrity!"

No one had ever told me that. I was proud of myself. He made me realize that I was strong. And that there were certain things that I just wouldn't do, no matter how desperate things seemed to be. In my mind, I was just being myself and sticking to my principles.

Altogether, my experience in that beautiful townhouse of his, with lovely mahogany leather furniture, warm afro-centric painted walls, scented oils and candles, and variety of plants adorning every corner of the house, was very educational. He advised me. He built my self-esteem. He cooked and cleaned. He treated me like a young African prince. And for the first time in my life, I was made to realize how beautiful of a man, both men and women thought I was. I am forever grateful for what The Lord taught me about myself at those early and vulnerable stages in my life.

Integrity. Honor. Humility. Confidence.

Living there also taught me to be more independent. I knew that it was time for me to break the cycle of moving from one friend's house to another. This was not the life that I had envisioned.

I started focusing more on negotiating and doing business online, while at his home. It was at his home, that I got my very first car. It was, if my memory serves me right, an old 1988 light brown, Toyota Camry. I found an Indiana University student selling it on the college online classified advertisement website. The student wanted close to $1000 dollars for his car. After more than a week of back to back negotiations with the student, The Lord had entered his heart and allowed him to sell me the car for only $150 dollars! I could not believe it. I was very happy with myself. I celebrated as if I had just won the lottery. This was a great accomplishment for me, and the mark of my freedom and independence in buying my very first car. It wasn't a fancy car, but that car symbolized the fact that, no longer would I have to beg and inconvenience my friends to borrow their car. To me, that car was as good as having a brand new Lamborghini. Slowly but surely, I was moving in the right direction and away from defeat!

I had been living with my new friend for about a month now. I had learned a lot. My mind had further expanded. Like a warm wind, passing through sprawling pastures on a pleasant summer day, it was time for me, once again, to move forward in my journey. It was time for me to travel back home and break the devastating news that I was facing 60 years in prison to my family.

Chapter 22

I sat on the plane, thousands of miles in the sky, staring out of the window and reflecting on where I was in life. I recall feeling a divine peace and calm throughout the travel. There was a sense of feeling that no matter what happened, everything would be alright.

When I arrived at my home in Irvington, New Jersey, my family welcomed me with a warm embrace. It had been so long since they had seen my face. I missed them dearly too. When I settled comfortably at home, I made it known to them that I had something very important to tell them all. My cousin and cousin in law, Hannah and Evan were coming over for dinner that night, so I decided to wait until they arrived, so that I could break the news to them all at once.

Throughout the day, the pressure was building. The anticipation was rising.

"What's the big news you have to tell us..?" my mom, sister and brother would ask me all throughout the day.

My dad, fortunately, was not around. He had traveled to Africa at the time I returned home. It would have been much more difficult and painful to break the news to both of my parents at the same time.

"Is it good news or bad news..?" they would ask.

Finally, late that evening, my cousin and cousin in law, Hannah and Evan had arrived. We all congregated, sitting comfortably in the living room. They waited eagerly to hear this important news that I had to tell them. Before I spoke, I wrestled whether I should start off by immediately telling them that I had been arrested for drug dealing and was facing 60 years in prison if convicted, and then telling them the entire story from beginning to end, that led me to that point, or, whether I should start the story from the very beginning, when I sold my first drug.

Either way, I knew that the news would be devastating and shocking. It was a matter of whether it would be worse to shock them in the beginning, or at the end. I chose the latter.

For the next hour, I invited my family into my secret world that I had been living in for the past year. I purged my entire heart into the living room that night. I took them on a journey through time. I remember the room being absolutely motionless and silent, throughout my confessions. There was a sad and somber feeling in the air as I spoke. And at the end of the story, there was much sorrow and many questions from my family. It seemed that the more I answered, the sadder the room became. I looked at my situation as the glass half full, however, my family could see no possible positive outcome of my circumstance.

Something this big, had never happened in our family before. Their son, brother, and cousin, who was supposed to be in college, studying medicine to become a doctor, was now facing what could be the rest of his life in jail.

I remember the look on my brother's face when the magnitude of my situation hit him. He let out a loud cry. Tears came pouring out of his eyes, as he repeatedly asked, "Why...?! Why...?!"

Why would I put myself in that situation? How could I be so selfish? How could I be so foolish? Within moments of seeing the sorrow, tears and pain from my older brother's face, I too broke down in cries. I had been so strong for all this time, since my arrest. But the love that I saw radiating from my older brother, as he cried for me...

I must pause from writing now, as the emotions race back to my heart...

I had realized... We both had realized... that there was a possibility that I would be separated for the rest of my life, from my best friend in the world. My virtually, twin brother, who I had been with, and known more than anyone else...who I grew up with in Germany and Africa, and loved unconditionally throughout my entire life, would have to live with the fact that I was a prisoner. We all hugged as my brother and I cried aloud that night, until there were no more tears left to cry.

"I'm not going to cry for you!" I vividly recall my mother telling me.

She refused. I couldn't blame her. She was absolutely shocked and disappointed by my foolish actions.

My mom begged me to stay home in New Jersey, and to request that my court case be transferred there, from Indiana. But my new home was Bloomington, Indiana. I had everything there. There was no way that I was going to leave. And with The Lord before me, I was ready to boldly battle my problems in Bloomington!

Chapter 23

So, against my mother's wishes, a few days later, I was back on the plane to my destiny! I can't remember exactly how, but by the grace of God, when I arrived back in Bloomington, I was able to raise enough money to rent a two bedroom apartment around campus.

It was called Woodlawn Apartments. I absolutely loved my new apartment. It was very simple. When you opened the apartment door, you walk into the living room. There was an amazingly beautiful, single, brick wall to your immediate right. Leading out of the living room was a sliding glass door that led to a patio with a view of a row of grass and the woods beyond a fence.

Sometimes, I would see deer approach the fence, just a few feet away from my first floor patio. Almost every morning, I had the heartwarming pleasure of watching chipmunks scurry across my patio. My kitchen had a nostalgic feel, with its old, rustic wooden cabinets.

Then, there were my two spacious bedrooms in the back. What a simple and humble apartment. There was no doubt that I was blessed. I didn't buy much furniture. I only bought a bed for my room and a futon for my living room. Whenever my friends stopped by to visit, which was very rare, I took out one or two foldable chairs. I remember having a small 13" inch screen television/video cassette recorder in one. I only had one movie virtually the entire year – "Billy Madison", starring the famous comedian actor, Adam Sandler. It's a story about a 27 year old son of a wealthy man, who decides to complete grades one through twelve, two weeks per grade, in order to prove to his father that he is worthy of inheriting his father's empire. It puts a smile on my face just to think about that movie. I must have watched it about a million times. After watching the movie a few dozen times, day after day, I could quote almost every line. That was what I usually did to entertain myself while in that apartment.

The apartment was just across the street from the main college mall, and just a few blocks walking distance from my best friends' apartment, who decided to live at the University Commons Apartment Complex for a second year.

It was perfect! I had an overall raised level of optimism and confidence when I returned from my trip from New Jersey. I was close to my best friends. I was within steps from the mall and grocery store. I had my very first car. And I was able to rent out a spacious two bedroom apartment for a very low price.

30,000 plus students were returning back to campus, so I knew that my herbal pill sales would go up eventually. Although there was still danger in selling them, in my mind, I thought to myself that I now had the green light to sell them, after the Bloomington Police had released me. I knew, however, that I had to be very careful with the words that I said from then on. It was confirmed that I was surely being closely watched.

But with my attitude, those were very happy days of my life. It seemed that, with a blink of an eye, I had gone from having nothing, and depending on others, to suddenly having all my needs provided for, overflowing, and in good measure! No longer did I have to beg my friends for favors. I had become highly independent. There was no doubt that Jesus Christ had turned the tides of misfortune away from me, and was now sending waves of blessings and favor, full speed into my direction.

The amazing thing, thinking back, is that I far from had it all. I certainly encountered stumbling blocks every day, during my third year in Bloomington, Indiana.

For one, there were some days that I had invested all my money on buying the herbal ecstasy pills, and had to go days without sufficient food until I was able to make a sale to a customer. Many days, especially earlier on in the year, I was forced to eat nothing but canned foods. My friends used to tease me when they found out that, at times, I had to drink sugar water. We always had a laugh about it.

Days that I ran out of milk for my cereal, you could find me in my quiet apartment eating cereal with water. Other days, I starved, knowing that the next day would be better. On many occasions, I had to remind myself that I was a survivor. I did what I had to do to manage, until I was able to find another buyer.

Perhaps, one main factor, outside of my immovable faith, that kept me going was the fact that I always had thousands of dollars of product that I knew would eventually sell, even if it meant drastically lowering my prices.

In addition, the tireless late hours that I was spending in front of the computer managing my online wholesale business was finally beginning to yield excellent profits.

So, all together, I was generating funds from multiple streams, including online sales, herbal pills, and selling apparel on consignment to local stores, shops in the mall, and barbershops and beauty shops. I also had a few shares of stocks in the stock market. I was extremely well hedged.

At only 19 years old, I had become a self-made hedge fund money manager, yet I had no idea. When you combine the planting of many seeds, with unshakable faith in Christ, there are no worries!

Suddenly, after a year of going to court every other month or so, the story that Joseph Diggs had told, that one fateful night at his home, was miraculously coming to fruition! The 60 years, and 3 separate drug charges that I was facing had miraculously been lowered to 40 years... then 30 years... then 20 years, with the possibility of dropping two of the three charges if I plead guilty to one! Hallelujah! The Lord's hand was at work! He was slashing my time from His throne in Heaven.

However, to me, 20 years in prison was the same as 60 years in prison. Each time that I would go to the court house, and my public defender would tell me the new offer of lower years in prison, my heart would silently rejoice.

Nevertheless, I stood my ground, and I always declined the offers. The Lord had planted it into my heart and mind to fight this battle to the very end! And as usual, once my heart and mind were set and full of immovable confidence, there was nothing in the natural world that could change it!

So many times, my public defender would advise and warn me to take a deal and plead guilty for my own good. I could hear him now.

"Maubrey, if I were you, I would plead guilty and take a deal for a reduced sentence. Going to jail for a few years is not the end of the world..."

He might as well have been speaking an alien language to me. As far as I was concerned, The Lord Jesus Christ had already punished, tested, and forgiven me fully for my sins. Christ told me in my spirit self, that I did not have to go to jail again. So, I placed all of my trust in Him. There was absolutely no way that any man could convince me otherwise. Not my lawyer, not my closest friends, not my family, not even myself, if I wanted to.

As my faith increased daily, so did knowledge and wisdom to make the right decisions increase. In the bottom of my heart, I imagined that in order to defeat this circumstance in my life, I would need to hire the best, and most expensive criminal lawyer in the state of Indiana – Brayden Miller.

After I had broken the news to my family and left New Jersey, my mother had made plans to fly down to Bloomington, Indiana to visit her son for the very first time, in the world that he called home and loved so much. It was just unfortunate that her first visit was for something like this. It had been over a year since my drug arrest now, and now, every court appointment could possibly be the trial. This could be the one, and she wanted to be there if it was. She also wanted to meet with this Brayden Miller, who was supposed to be the best attorney around.

So, together with my amazing Aunt Hailey, who had flown in from London, England to New Jersey, just days before, they both arrived in the tiny, secret little town of Bloomington, Indiana for the first time in their lives. Despite the circumstances that I was in, I remember being so excited that they were coming into my bubble of a world that I lived in.

I recall having to shut down my entire herbal ecstasy selling operation for that week that they were there. Although I had told them in New Jersey that I was caught and released the second time for selling the herbals, needless to say, my family was not the least bit happy that I was dealing anything that could be mistaken as illegal in any sense. They warned me to stop before I departed New Jersey.

Before they came, I remember thinking long and hard, where to hide the herbal powder and capsules. Should I hide them in my car? No, that wasn't safe. In my mailbox? No, I couldn't take a chance. Somewhere in the kitchen? That would have been a bad idea. I could see my mom and aunt getting ready to cook a big meal for me, and finding kilograms of powder, then doing who knows what with it. There was no one that I felt I could trust enough to hold that amount of product for a week. There were no good hiding places in my practically empty apartment. So, I simply wrapped the powder and capsules in a plastic bag and hid it in my suitcase, underneath all my clothes.

I could not imagine my mom or aunt having any rational reason to open my suitcase in my room. I got into my old, $150 dollar car and went to pick them up. As usual, it was always a joyful and happy occasion to see my mom and my aunt. We told jokes the entire ride to my apartment. My mom had never seen her baby boy drive before, and the car was so ancient, we couldn't help but to have laughs during the entire ride. I knew that they were just so happy to see me in my environment, and that I was at least settled and happy, despite my seemingly grave circumstance.

I invited my best friends over to meet my mom and aunt. My friends were curious and excited to see where such a unique, unusually happy, and weird boy came from. I was happy to show my mom and aunt my wonderful circle of friends that had supported, helped, and stuck by me the entire time. We had many laughs when my friends came over.

Also, I can't forget how humbled I was by the compliments that my friends were giving me to my mom, saying that her son was a good person and friend. It put a lot into perspective for me and gave me further confidence that I was moving in the right direction in life, despite my many faults and bad decisions.

Shortly after that day, my mom, Aunt Hailey, and I were in the court house. The trial date had been continued, postponed once again. I breathed a sigh of relief. I knew that the more months the case dragged on, the closer I was to victory.

We immediately made an appointment to meet with the best attorney around. My mom, my aunt, the attorney, and I sat for some time in a private conference room, discussing my case. In the end, the cost to hire him was a minimum of $10,000 dollars, and even more if I decided to take my case to trial. I remember when my mom asked the attorney how much his services would cost. Just like I had seen on television in the past, instead of him saying his fee out loud, he slid a piece of paper in front of him, toward his body, then quietly wrote down the figure "$10,000" on the paper, then slid it in the direction of my mom and Aunt Hailey. I laughed inside. I had never seen anyone do that in real life. It reminded me almost of the way I would handle my past drug transactions.

I imagined that my mom alone could not afford that kind of money. She said she would talk it over with the family and get back to him. It didn't look as if we were going to be able to hire him. However, I wasn't discouraged. That day, I said to myself, that if I was going to hire him for sure, then I would have to raise a large portion of the funds myself. Or, I would have to boost my level of faith, and trust in Christ to deliver me through this case without a hired attorney. I chose the latter.

Things were flowing smoothly during my mom and Aunt Hailey's stay in Bloomington. I had been doing a good job in keeping my herbal sales business away from them, until one day, when I returned home from running an errand. My mom revealed to me that she had discovered my bundle of herbal powder and capsules in my suitcase. My heart jumped immediately! The very first thing I thought was that "I really hope that she did not flush thousands and thousands of dollars worth of powder down the toilet." The second thought that naturally came to mind was, "How in the world did she find it under the pile of clothes in my suitcase?" I already knew the answer to that question. Like any concerned mother, whose son was living alone with no regular job and facing a drug trial, she must have searched my entire apartment looking for drugs the first opportunity that she got.

I could not blame her. Perhaps, I would have done the same thing if I had a child in a similar situation. I thought fast.

"Mom..." I said nonchalantly, "It's my workout supplemental meal powder. I take it after my workouts."

Fortunately, I had a few powder supplement containers in the apartment, to corroborate my story.

"So, what about all those capsules?" my mom inquired.

"Oh, I put the powder in them sometimes..." I quickly lied again.

I had managed to change what seemed so obvious to be drugs, to workout powder supplements. I'm sure she had her doubts, however she had no choice but to let the issue go.

I remember thinking, "I sure hope that she doesn't ask me to mix a spoon full of the powder in water, and drink it in front of her and Aunt Hailey."

A spoon full would have been about ten pills worth. Under normal circumstances, I believe she would have asked me to. However, she likely decided that the less she worried, the better. The issue was closed.

My mom and Aunt Hailey stayed for a few more days until it was time for them to depart. Once again, it was back to business for me! It was back to marketing and selling my legal drugs. It was back to spending all day and night in front of my computer, building my online business.

Chapter 24

As I sit here writing in this library's computer lab in Belleville, New Jersey, during this month of miracles, just four days after Christmas of 2009, and at the dawn of a new decade, I have just now realized the significance of what The Lord Jesus Christ has been stirring my heart and mind, for the past few days – The Code of Life: 1+2=3. How simple in form and structure. How obvious and clear from the beginning of wisdom and education. 1+2=3. Perhaps, my undying love of children, combined with my continuous, unyielding prayers for unlimited and infinite, divine wisdom has led me to this revelation! How pure it is. The Code of Life: 1+2=3. So simple. So true! You have 1. And you need to get to 3. Simply do 2!

Rewinding back in time, it was back to nonstop hustling all week, then partying all night with girls and my best friends during the weekends. Every day was filled with excitement! Every day was a rush! There was never a dull moment in Maubrey's life! Time was flying by faster than the speed of the earth circling the sun. Each day taught me new grains of lessons. Yet another letter from the court had come in the mail that I had to appear to what was supposed to be my trial date.

This time, just shortly after my mom and aunt flew to Bloomington, Indiana from New Jersey, my mom and dad came to accompany me in court. This was the first time in the three years, since I had left home to college, that my dad had come to visit me in Indiana. On what was to be my day of destiny, my mom, dad, and I said a deep prayer, and then, we were on our way to the court house!

Once again, my emotions overtake me. I must pause to gather myself. I am taken back to that exact moment of time, as I again, fight back a flood of tears of joy and happiness from overflowing from the banks of my eyes.

For over a year, before that day, I had been through so much. I had journeyed much a distance. I had held on so tightly, to my immovable belief and faith in what The Lord was quietly whispering into my heart – to what Christ had been instructing me to do, when the world was telling me opposite. The world was telling me to do the safe thing. The world was telling me to do the commonsensical thing – to plead guilty, and serve a few years in prison, instead of risking 60 years in prison. The world, including my friends and family had my best interest in heart. Their advice and warnings were meant to protect me. However, they did not fully understand what I understood. They did not fully understand that I had The Ultimate Protector! El Shaddai...Jehovah Jireh...The Rock and The Fortress...The Deliverer...The Righteous Judge...The Truth…The Prince of Peace…The One Savior…The Alpha and Omega! Jesus Christ!

Together as a powerful force, one by one, my mom, dad and I walked through the metal detectors of the court house, covered with the blood of Jesus and surrounded by the invisible force field of God!

When we entered my public defender's office, he told us that the trial date would be continued once again. We then spoke about my case briefly. He touched base with me, as to where I was, concerning whether I still wanted to take my seemingly hopeless case to trial. He advised my parents that I could serve many years in jail, and that there was a strong and likely chance that a jury would find me guilty during a trial.

Still, the decision was entirely mine. I told him that I was certain that I wanted to take my case to trial. As usual, I was looked at as if I were crazy.

Suddenly, my public defender uttered words to me, in front of my parents that I will never forget!

"If we can get the prosecutors to agree to lower your charges so that you serve no time in jail, get placed on probation, and only do a few hours of community service, would you take it?"

How powerful The Lord Jesus is! How marvelous ways He performs! I did not show any excitement on my face. I turned to the left and then to the right, looking my parents in the eyes. At that moment in time, everyone in the room knew what was transpiring before our eyes. There was such an electric energy in the air. You could feel it in your bones!

"Yes. I can consider it." I said, after turning my face back toward my public defender.

Was this what The Lord wanted for me? Was this the miracle that I had been believing and praying so diligently for? My public defender left the office, then some time later, returned with news!

"Maubrey," my attorney announced, "The prosecution has agreed to drop your case today! They will place you on probation and give you a number of hours of community service, if you sign paperwork pleading guilty. You'll serve no time in jail!"

Wow! I get chills! Hallelujah! I had been teleported to a new dimension! From facing 60 years in prison, to now a few hours of community service! What an awesome God we serve!

But again, I remained calm, and showed no excitement on my face, however, inside my body, there was jubilant celebration! My lawyer handed the paperwork to me, then instructed my parents and me to follow him out of his office, directing us how to get to the room that we were to meet him in, downstairs in the basement of the court house. We would be briefed on all the details of my probation and my plea deal.

He took a separate elevator. As I walked with my parents, a powerful force came over me. It was The Lord again...! The Lord was telling my spirit that this was a miracle indeed, but that I had not seen a fraction of His amazing wonders yet! The Lord told me, to the surprise and disbelief of my parents, that I should not sign those papers! And as The Lord spoke to my conscience, my decision was made! My mind was set!

When my parents and I got downstairs to reunite with my public defender, I told him that I would like to take the paperwork, which was about 20 pages thick, home and read it over. There were a few other people in the office looking on. They may have been members of the prosecution team. It made me feel as if they were waiting to witness me sign my life away. I felt a bit uneasy. After I said that I'd like to think it over at home, before signing, that is when my public defender and the others in the room revealed their impatience and frustration.

"Just sign it... Just sign it now!" I recall them repeating. "You don't need to take it home...!"

Everyone was talking so fast to me. They spoke to me in such an urgent tone. Throughout, I remained extremely calm.

"I understand," I said, "But I'd have to take it home and read everything carefully."

Their frustration grew stronger. By this time, my parents, who strongly disagreed with my decision just a few minutes earlier, had realized the method to my madness. We had never in our lives seen anyone this anxious and forceful to convince someone to sign paperwork. It could only mean one thing. The Lord was going to deliver me completely from this fiery tribulation!

And the prosecutors sensed it, and wanted to at least convince me to plead guilty before it was too late. The prosecutors and my public defender were ready to end this year long, exhausting case!

That afternoon, in that courthouse, my faith in The Lord Jesus Christ grew to another level! What an optimistic and victorious ride back to my apartment that was!

Soon, all my family and friends discovered the good news! It was quite a day of celebration. Suddenly, with a blink of an eye, my parents, friends, and family finally realized the magnificent power of what I had been preaching all along! They had witnessed, firsthand, the glory of unmoving faith in action!

In just over a year, I went from being a man facing up to 60 years in prison, to a man facing probation and community service! Suddenly, my family and friends' doubts, worries, and disbeliefs, turned into clear optimism and hope. Their well intending reasons to convince me to plead guilty and serve a few years in prison, suddenly turned into them telling me statistics and reasons why there was no chance I would be found guilty.

I needed not convincing. I was convinced from the very beginning. However, no one believed that 60 could possibly turn to 0! It is amazing how persistent faith and proof can instantly change the minds of people.

Nevertheless, to the world, I had taken a huge gamble with my life and my future in declining the offer. The battle was far from over! It wasn't before long until friends and family began attempting to convince me to agree to the offer. How quickly man forgets. It was as if I was offered guaranteed trillions of dollars to go against the seed that The Lord had buried deep in the ocean floor of my heart, but my faith in The Lord Jesus was telling me to take a chance, risking losing trillions, in order to receive infinite and unlimited divine wealth. The choice was clear as water. I would continue following the still, small voice of The Lord!

Chapter 25

My parents flew back home, and I was back to my adventurous life and on my own once more. Time seemed to have flown by during the months after. Throughout the remainder of my third year in Bloomington, I continued to receive letters in the mail, informing me that my trial date had been set. Each time I would go, I was told that the date had been postponed again.

And as winter turned to spring, my public defender continued attempting to convince me to accept the guilty plea. My answers remained the same.

Before I knew it, the school year had ended, and I found myself outside my apartment building, loading all my possessions into a rented truck. Just a month or two before my apartment lease expired, I had been evicted again for late payments. I had accumulated thousands and thousands of dollars in inventory and products, however, I never kept much cash around. I always immediately reinvested my money. I could never bare the thought of spending money, when I knew that it could be multiplied. The second that I had money, it was as good as gone. I had become so accustomed to this money management method. Many times, I even compromised my hunger. It may not have been the best practice, but it worked for me at the time.

As I packed my possessions out of my apartment and into the rented truck, I reminisced about all the fond and memorable moments that I experienced in that warm, rustic, two bedroom apartment. I thought about the time that I was about to go over to my friend and former supplier's apartment and fight him after he had disrespected me on the phone because I owed him about $1000 dollars. I remember getting all dressed up in about three layers of fighting clothes, wearing high knee, bright blue, old football socks, putting Vaseline all over my face, and shadow boxing in my apartment to prepare. It was really a comical sight to see, now that I think of it. Perhaps, I was really insulted by how he spoke to me on the phone, or perhaps, it had been almost four years since I had fought someone, and I just wanted to fight to get it out of my system and prove to myself that I still had it.

I recall storming into my best friends' apartment telling them, including Landon, who was also my former supplier's friend, and the one who introduced me to him, that I was going to fight him. An hour or so later, we were all laughing as usual, and I had changed my mind.

As I loaded the rented moving truck, I also remembered the time that one of my other best friends in my circle had gotten in a fatal car accident while racing cars late at night. By the grace of God, he himself survived. The news was broadcasted on many national television news programs including CNN. It was such a surreal experience for me. I had never had to visit a friend in the hospital until that tragic event. We used to ride in a car as a group to visit him and the other survivors in the hospital. I vividly remember listening to the late rapper, Tupac's new single during every ride to the hospital, that ironically, had come out at the time of the accident. The title of Tupac's song was "Dying to live". Looking back, I truly believe that The Lord used that song to get us through that tragic and humbling time in our lives, and to bring us closer together as friends. That experience certainly made us realize how fragile life truly was.

And then, I couldn't forget the time that I became unbearably ill with mononucleosis, also called "mono", or the "kissing disease", a common viral illness that can leave you feeling tired, weak and debilitated for weeks or months. I had no idea what had hit me.

Days before, as usual, I was at a house party on campus and I locked lips with an attractive girl that I was dancing with. Little did I know that I wouldn't be able to function normally for the next few weeks. This was like no cold or fever that I had ever experienced in my life! My throat was extremely sore. I had a high fever for many days. My glands and tonsils became swollen. And worst of all, I was so weak and fatigued, that I was bed ridden for weeks. I've never been one to go to hospitals. I fought through the pain for weeks.

Then finally, one night, around 2am in the morning, alone in my dark apartment, I was suddenly awoken in a cold sweat. My glands and tonsils became completely swollen, restricting my breathing. I sat up in bed gasping for air. My illness had peaked! In a panicked rush, I quickly called my mother in New Jersey. She urged me to go to the hospital immediately. I honestly did not think that I would make it that night! I knew that I could not afford to call for an ambulance. I decided to attempt to drive almost a half an hour away to Bloomington Hospital.

Weaker than I had ever been in my life, that night, I literally crawled out of my bed, put on some shoes and a jacket, and struggled my way to my car.

My time was running out! Late that night, with the streets virtually empty, I raced to the hospital. The more I drove, the more I could not breathe.

"Am I going to die before I reach the hospital!?" I thought to myself.

I asked The Lord to give me the strength to make it.

Finally, in my old maroon Toyota, I came storming into the emergency room parking lot. I parked crookedly directly in front of the emergency room entrance, and poured out of my car. Completely out of breath and gasping for air, with a dazed look on my face, with sweat seeping through the pores of my forehead, in the hoarsest of voices, I exclaimed to the hospital receptionist that I could not breathe and that I needed a doctor immediately!

That was the night that I discovered that there was a "kissing illness" called "mono"! I was prescribed antibiotics, and I was back to my normal self days later.

What a lesson that was for me! God was telling me that I should slow down, to be very careful, and use more discretion before engaging in passionate, sweet kisses with women, no matter how beautiful they were. The Lord certainly has a funny and interesting way of teaching me lessons. As a father with a sense of humor, who thinks of clever ways to teach his son a lesson, I could see The Lord in Heaven with a grin on His face. Another valuable lesson learned!

Next, I recalled the time that I fronted a past drug client a few hundred legal herbal ecstasy capsules. Business had been slow for a few weeks, so I decided that if I fronted some capsules to someone that I sensed that I could trust to sell them and pay me back, then I would soon reap the rewards. It had been days since I heard from or spoke to the person that I fronted the pills to. I figured that, as usual, he was selling the capsules and making a lot of money. I called him. Unfortunately, he reported bad news to me when we spoke on the phone. He said that he had gotten complaints and that his main customer, who he was going to sell it to said that the capsules were not genuine ecstasy. I was not worried or surprised by this news.

By then, I had realized that many of my customers had doubts about the authenticity of the herbs, however because the effects of the herbs were so potent and similar to the actual drugs, they would eventually take them or sell them.

He wanted to return the hundreds of capsules that I had fronted him. That was definitely not what I wanted. He called my cell phone a few more times after that conversation. I purposely did not pick up his calls. I was hoping that he would eventually decide to sell them.

After about a week, I finally called him. To my disappointment, and deservingly, he told me on the phone in a very confrontational manner, that he had thrown the capsules away in a brook, after I had ignored his numerous calls. I was extremely upset and insulted. I could not believe that anyone would throw away hundreds of hallucinogens in a brook.

Many thoughts went through my mind. One was that he may have been an informant working with the police to arrest me. And that when they tested the herbs and found out that they were not illegal drugs, their plan had backfired, and instructed him to return the pills to me. Perhaps, when the police realized what I was trying to do in my staling, they instructed him to say that he had thrown them away, in order to get me to threaten him on the phone, or do something illegal to get my money from him.

Next, I thought that, like a few of my customers, he thought that I was the one who was attempting to set him up with the police by having him hold on to that many drugs for so long. So he decided to destroy any evidence by throwing the capsules in a brook. That made sense to me too.

Or perhaps, he was not working with the police, nor did he think I was, and that he decided to keep the pills after he realized that I was not picking up his phone calls. Either way, I made it clear to him on the phone, without making obvious threats, just in case our conversations were being recorded by the police, that there would be problems if he did not return my capsules or pay me a few thousand dollars for them.

I called him numerous times for days. This time, he was the one ignoring my calls. This type of pressure would have worked and had worked in the past, with most college students, who owed me money, and had a lot to lose. However, this person was different. He was not a student, had a rough demeanor, and had nothing to lose.

Finally, after many calls, he picked up the phone, and after exchanging harsh words, he threatened that if I called him again, he would "put a bullet between my eyes!" Wow! No one had ever threatened me with those words before. The thought of a bullet going between my eyes was not at all pleasant to me.

After he had abruptly hung up the phone on me, I furiously called him many more times that hour. He did not answer. After I calmed my nerves, I thought about it. No matter how I looked at the situation, the tension and friction was caused by me. It was completely my fault. I decided to swallow my pride, take the loss, and let it go.

From the very beginning, I have always understood the simple principle that the business, and making money was always more important than getting violent. That understanding is one of the reasons that made me last as a drug dealer for so long. Conflict and violence is never the answer! There is always a wiser way to solve problems – God's way.

Almost finished moving out early that day, I laughed inside as I recalled the many times that I turned down thousands of dollars, because I sensed that the telephone conversation was being taped by the Bloomington Police Department. By then, I knew and immediately recognized the speech patterns, the stuttering, and the nervousness of past and new customers who were attempting to betray me. I certainly had no clients in Bloomington that were Oscar winning actors.

Standing outside in the ever familiar parking lot on that warm, sunny day, of course, I could not forget how nice the apartment management women were to me during my stay. Almost every month, as usual, I would be a few days or weeks late on my rent. I was thankful that they were so kind, always worked with me, and gave me time.

What an amazing year it had been living in that cozy apartment. I had learned many valuable lessons and had been through many experiences. Despite the ups and downs, I would not have changed a single detail.

I loaded the last of my possessions into the rented moving truck, took a final look at the old apartment complex, took a deep breath, and drove away from my past. Where would the journeys of life take me? I had no idea. I was sailing the winds of my destiny! Once again, having nowhere to live, and no set plans, I drove to a local storage company a few miles away, and loaded all of my possessions, including the herbal drugs, into storage.

Next, I went to my best friends', Gavin, Landon, and Gabriel's apartment, to be around some positive energy, and to gather my thoughts together to decide what I was going to do next.

I had a burning feeling though, of where my journey was inevitably going to take me next. The feeling had passed my mind many times in the weeks leading to that day. There was still no way that I was going to concede, and give up my dreams of getting re-enrolled into my dream school, Indiana University. There was absolutely no possibility of me packing up all my possessions and traveling back home to New Jersey.

I could not stay at my best friends' apartment and have them risk getting evicted, especially after what had happened the previous year. I was a new man. I was now a self-efficient man. I was now an independent man. My friends knew it, compared to how dependent I was on them for many things during the first two years in Bloomington. I had been through so much in the past year, that there was no way that I could go back to leaning on my friends again.

I spent the majority of the day with my friends at their apartment, pondering, from time to time, whether I was really going to do it. After all, I had a contact list of friends that I could call and easily be offered a place to stay for the summer.

Then later that evening, the time for procrastination, doubt, and hesitation was over! I told Landon that I was ready for him to give me a ride to the homeless shelter!

On the way there, we made jokes about how it was going to be for me in the shelter. Landon knew that I was strong. Landon knew that I was a natural survivor. By then, he had witnessed me escape so many seemingly impossible circumstances. He may have not known how, but I believe that he knew that I would eventually get out of this situation too.

It was on that very ride to the shelter, that I first knew for sure that I would eventually have a testimony to tell to generations in the future! I knew that my life was very unique. I knew that The Lord was putting me through many obstacles and delivering me through the flames without a single burn, but stronger than I had entered, in order to be an inspiration to the masses!

Late that night, we finally arrived at the small one story shelter. Adjacent to the shelter was the community soup kitchen. This was it! I was actually going to go through with it! I looked Landon in the eye, as a soldier would look at a great comrade before going in to war. We shook hands, said "goodbye", then I exited his car.

Landon watched waiting, as I was admitted into the shelter. Afterward, I looked back and watched him drive away into the night. I was far from sad or down. Ironically, I was actually the most optimistic and confident about my future, than I had ever been in my life. I knew that the only place to go from that moment was up! I knew that I would, in due time, "bounce back" in a most magnificent way! And most importantly of all, I had a vision and a plan of action.

With the cash that I had, the quantity of herbs in storage, and the negotiation and bargaining skills that I had developed since early youth, my plan was to go to the Indiana University online classified advertisement website, day in, and day out, buying out everything that the students were trying to sell before they left town. I was going to spend every day making offers, driving to students' apartments, and buying whatever they had for sale in order to sell them months later, for huge profits, when the students returned for the next school year. I was going to go on a buying spree. I would buy furniture, leather sofas, cars, electronics, stereo systems, televisions, microwave ovens, video game consoles, PlayStation I's, PlayStation II's, Microsoft Xboxes, DVD players and VCRs. I would buy twin, full, queen, and king sized beds. If it could be resold, I would buy it!

That would mean that I would not have much spending money at my disposal, and that I would have to stay in the shelter for longer than I would have wanted. But as I had done many times in my life, I was willing to suffer greatly to achieve my dreams. If you have a great dream, you must be willing and prepared to suffer greatly! Also, I needed a break from the world that I was living in. I had mentally and spiritually prepared myself.

Chapter 26

I brought nothing with me to the homeless shelter, but the burning fire in my heart and a believing spirit. I walked through the doors of that shelter with the shield of Christ surrounding me! As I walked into the doors, to my immediate left was the registration office. Directly in front of me was a door that led to a long, narrow hallway. To my right was the television, recreation room. Further down the hallway, to the left, was the kitchen. Then further along the left side of the hallway were the showers. On the right side, and to the end of the narrow hallway were the separate men's and women's sleeping and living quarters. It was not as bad as I had imagined. They took me in warmly and welcomed me.

The place was very clean. It had no bad odors. And everything seemed peaceful and organized. The presence of Christ was certainly with me. After I filled out all the necessary forms, and was told the rules, I was given clean white sheets, a warm blanket, and a pillow. I was put in a room to the right side of the narrow hallway and assigned one of the top bunk beds. It felt as if I was in summer camp again. Only this time, I had no idea who my five or six other roommates were. I climbed up to my bed, rested my head on my pillow, closed my eyes, and went into a deep sleep.

My daily routine in the homeless shelter consisted of me, along with the others, being awoken very early in the morning to shower and brush our teeth. We were then made to leave the shelter to go to a local church on campus, a few miles away, to get breakfast. After having breakfast at the church, I worked on the computer for hours, in the Indiana University Library, until early afternoon, when we had to return to the shelter for lunch. If I missed the scheduled lunch, for any reason, then I would have to wait until lunch the next day. Needless to say, with my appetite, I can't recall ever missing lunch.

There was always about an hour or two of down time between finishing breakfast at the church and the time when the library opened, that was just around the corner from the church. That hour or two each morning, sitting on the pavement of the sidewalk, made me truly realize the gravity of my situation. I was really a homeless person! I was really on my own! I had nowhere to go, and no one to turn to but my Lord, God.

I was more determined than ever! I never changed my loose fitting, denim, Abercrombie and Fitch jeans. I rotated shirts and underwear daily, and I washed my clothes at my best friends' apartment. After wearing the same jeans for weeks straight, they began to tear in the knee area and the rear area. I didn't care. I continued to wear them as they were, as a style. I had many jeans in storage. However, that wasn't the point. Strangers even offered to donate gently used jeans to me. I humbly declined the offers. I had set in my mind that I was not going to change my jeans, no matter how torn they became, until I left the shelter! I would use that as a motivating force to leave the shelter.

After lunch, I would usually go right back to the library to work on the computer. Then we would have to return to the shelter and sign in before our curfew, early in the evening.

Finally, I would lay in my top bunk bed, visualizing, dreaming, planning, and listening to music for some time, before finally going to sleep. The next day, it was the same routine over again.

After about a week in the shelter, I started working out and training again. I had made up my mind that, despite how bad my situation looked in the natural, and how impossible it may seem to the outside world, I was going to reenroll into Indiana University and get on the football team and back on the wrestling team.

From that small homeless shelter, a new seed was born! I ran miles under the hot summer's sun. I did hundreds of pushups daily. I ate very well. I borrowed friends' school identification cards to get into the Indiana University recreational center. Week after week, my body rapidly began to transform for the better. Now, at 20 years old, standing 5' 10" inches tall, and weighing close to 170 pounds, I was metamorphosing from a man of above average shape, to a man in peak physical stature.

My friends used to wonder how... how a guy living in a homeless shelter could have so much hope, enthusiasm, and excitement for life. But really, nothing about me had changed. I had been the same optimistic Maubrey all my life. The only difference now, was that, to the outside world, I was facing a seemingly insurmountable hurdle. With the daily routine that I kept, and the continuous happiness on my face, there was no way you could know that I was a man living in a homeless shelter, and facing 60 years in prison.

That homeless shelter could have either been my downfall, or it could have been the stepping stone that would catapult me into new levels. I chose to make it my stepping stone!

Within just two weeks of living in the shelter, I had already bought and sold thousands of dollars of products. I was working harder than I had ever worked before. My storage unit was filling up daily, in preparation of me selling everything at summer's end, when the students returned to campus.

Soon, I was driving two cars! I negotiated and bought my second car for about $200 dollars, roughly 75% off of what it was worth. I was truly being blessed magnificently, while living in the shelter. In the shelter, if you had a working cell phone, you were looked at in high regards. But if you had both a cell phone and a car for transportation, as I did, you were treated like royalty. You might as well have been a billionaire!

It was a very interesting observation. In my other life on campus, no one would think anything of having two old cars, but in this new world that I was in, those old cars that I had was looked upon as gold.

Soon, I was giving rides to fellow shelter mates. It gave me the opportunity to get to bond with and know many of them. I quickly realized that we were all good people. We just made a few mistakes and wrong decisions that ended us up in the shelter. They all showed me much love and honor, just as my fellow inmates did during my two weeks in prison.

Finally, after an entire month of patiently living in the homeless shelter, Christ stepped in! He decided that it was time for His child to be promoted! He decided that I had passed the test of faith!

Miraculously, a student, who conveniently, was leaving Indiana for the summer to work in Newark, New Jersey, a town bordering my hometown of Irvington, New Jersey, agreed to let me sublease her furnished room in a multiple occupancy, colonial styled home for only $75 dollars for the month and a half left before the Indiana University fall semester began! We certainly made an immediate connection since we had something in common to relate to.

Only $75 dollars for an entire month and a half! And what a beautiful part of campus that was. It was just around the corner from the library that I had been attending daily. I later found out from the landlord, that many decades ago, that very house was home to the president of Indiana University.

As The Lord did to Joseph, by promoting him from a prisoner in the land of Egypt, to living in quarters where past rulers lived, with a turn of a key, The Lord had caused His child to be delivered out of the confines of a homeless shelter, to living in quarters of former presidents!

Once more, I can feel the tears of joy rising to my eyes, as I relive that miraculous part of my life. I realize that it is no wonder that I am such a stout believer. I have seen the first hand proof of Christ's works so many times in my life. I am a living and perpetual testimony of the wonders of His glory! Living in that homeless shelter was, without a doubt, one of the most humbling experiences of my life.

Chapter 27

My journey to The Kingdom continued once more. Once again, I had a beautiful, cozy place of my own that I could call home. With my new home being just a few blocks from the student nightclubs and bars, it was time for me to celebrate my meaningful accomplishment! It was time for me to show my face to the world once again! I was a renaissance man – a new and reborn man!

Going out at night, and interacting with my friends, I could feel an undeniable glow around my body. My clothes were new! My smile was brighter. My eyes shined with happiness. I radiated with positivity. I had just been saved! I was in my secret dwelling place!

It is amazing. During the time that I was living in the homeless shelter, there was a hit song by rapper, Juvenile, one of the former members of the Hot Boys, the rap group that reignited my love for music, years before in high school. The title of the song was "Bounce Back". In essence, the song was about bouncing back from adversity. I used that song as a powerful motivational influence in getting out of the shelter. While living in the shelter, every time I visited my other African friends' home, I would always walk in with a smile on my face, nodding my head and chanting the chorus: "I'm 'bout to bounce back... I'm 'bout to bounce back... I'm 'bout to bounce back...". It always lifted the spirit of the entire room and put a smile on my African friends' face to see that someone living in a homeless shelter could have so much hope.

Now that I had made it out of the shelter, and finally had a place of my own, I had accomplished what I had been chanting over and over again for weeks! I had certainly "bounced back"!

Around the same time, a hit song by Mase, a rapper who had left the music industry to become a minister of Christ, and had returned to the music industry was also on the television and radio all the time. The title of his comeback song was "Welcome Back". And every time my African friends, that were from Zambia, Mali, and Kenya would see me pull up in one of my now, three different cars, they would all, with bright smiles on their faces, cheerfully sing in unison to me, "Welcome back...Welcome back-Welcome back-Welcome back..." It was an amazing feeling, how much those two songs meant to me. They seemed to have entered the world, and into my life, at just the right time.

Just because I had been delivered out of the homeless shelter, did not mean that I could rest on my laurels. I fully understood that if I was not only going to survive, but prosper abundantly, I would have to stay absolutely focused! I was back to business! I was back to socializing! I was back to being my true self!

Between my online business, the clothing stores on and around campus, that I was supplying clothes and accessories to, the herbals that I had, the three cars, the jewelry, the thousands of dollars in furniture and electronics that I had invested in, and the stocks that I owned, I was very well hedged.

One day, in my room by myself, I looked around. Then it all hit me! I was surrounded by everything that I needed. My room looked like a secret hidden cave of treasures.

Then, another day, as I laid there on a king sized bed, in a small space, between the wall and a stack of other smaller sized beds, piled high to the ceiling, with the local radio station playing soft music in the background, and warmth of the summer's heat radiating in my room, I fell into a deep sleep. I had an amazingly pleasant dream. When I awoke, The Lord had revealed to me my new last name... DESTINED! Maubrey Destined! At that very moment, I was one million percent sure why I was sent to this world – that I was Destined to change the world for the better! For the first time in my life, Christ had made it crystal clear to me.

Just days later, I tattooed the name "DESTINED", in biblical font letters, from top to bottom, along the side of my muscle-toned right arm. It is a constant reminder of who and what I truly am, never forgetting the mission that I was sent here to complete.

Months later, my new name, Maubrey Michael Destined, became official, and was legally changed. Ever since being delivered from jail, that fateful Sunday night, I had a burning desire to change my name. I knew that I was a chosen, renewed and blessed man. And I knew that my name should be changed. Throughout the year, from time to time, I would think about different surnames. I thought a few names were good, however, they just weren't the one. I know now, that it was not up to me to choose my new name. But I had to be patient, and be put through, and pass a few more tests by The Lord, in order to qualify myself for this new name.

Just as God had forgiven and changed the murderer, Saul's name to Paul, in The Holy Bible, God had forgiven and anointed me with my new name as my eyes opened.

Maubrey Destined!

Living in that small, single room house of presidents was truly a time of miracles, visions, breakthroughs, and enlightenments. I used to listen to music and just stare out of my window, at the beautiful scene of the street. Sometimes, I would sit in one of my cars and listen to music for long periods of time. I was truly at peace during that stage in my life. It was also in that room that I raised the strength to do over 80 pushups for the first time in my life. I was breaking personal barriers and limitations. I was moving forward in life.

Soon, I went to the Indiana University financial aid and bursar office to find out whether I qualified for any loans or grants. I was approved for a few thousand dollars. But it was far from enough to cover the roughly $30,000 dollars it would cost to re-enroll in school. I begged them to allow me to enroll back into classes for the upcoming school year. I told them that I had a business, and would pay my tuition by the end of the year. By the grace of God, they agreed! They had nothing to lose. If I could not pay, then it was my time that I was wasting, and I would not get the credits. I did not care. It was a step forward in the right direction! I was determined to pay for my schooling.

Before I knew it, time had flown like swift winds through the sails of a boat. My sublease in the former president's quarters had expired. I had less than 48 hours to move my vast amount of merchandise and furniture out of the house. Once again, going with the flow of Jesus as usual, I had made no definite previous arrangements.

With my bare hands, and with the help of generous students in the house from time to time, I emptied the room of all the beds, couches, electronics, televisions, laptops, and household appliances out to the front of the house that evening. I remember it as if it were yesterday. Thousands of dollars worth of investments that I had collected throughout the entire summer, just laying out there on the sidewalk. I can vividly see the image, as I had to sit there all night on the front porch, watching my possessions, so that they didn't get stolen or vandalized. I could feel the heaviness of my eyelids, as I struggled to stay awake past the wee hours of the night sky. I stared at the stars from time to time, wondering if I had the strength to make it. I watched night critters scurry down the street and sidewalk every so often. I felt the cool chill of the midnight's summer breeze. I watched drunkard students pass by on their way from the nearby bars and clubs. I daydreamed about my coming future. I dozed off many times, but was awoken by my conscience telling me that I could not risk having anything go wrong by falling asleep, after all that diligent work I had done the entire summer. Thousands of dollars were at stake!

After yet another doze, my eyes were awoken to the feel of morning dew in the air and by the sounds of birds chirping, ready for their first meal of the day. How majestic it was to awake after sleeping outdoors, early that morning. Bloomington had never looked so beautiful!

When afternoon arrived, it was time for action! That was the day that the students were moving back into campus from all over the country. I was fortunate that the house was located on a very popular side street. Car after car drove by. I had drawn a huge "for sale" sign for by-passers to clearly see. Hour after hour, the money started pouring in! I was giving deals and discounts to students left and right. It gave me great joy to see the smiles on their faces after I had saved most of them hundreds of dollars from not having to purchase from stores. I made many friends that day.

By mid afternoon, I could not contain all the money in my pocket. All the work, time and energy that I had invested in was beginning to pay off handsomely. It was truly a feeling of accomplishment. Under the hot sun, I helped students move the heavy furniture into their apartments, while asking their roommates and friends to watch my possessions while I was gone. I had trust, and I would do anything, and go out of my way to make the sale happen.

Within 24 hours, I had sold out! I now had thousands of dollars in my bank account! I was back! Yet again, it was my time to move forward in my journey. I took one final look at that house of presidents, nodded my head with respect and acknowledgment of what Christ had done for me in my short time living there. I thanked Christ, and drove away. Where was I driving to? I had bigger dreams now! Bigger goals! I was moving to The Boulders!

Chapter 28

The Boulders apartment complex was truly the finest living residences around campus. It was such a higher standard of living. The Boulders apartment complex was in a peaceful, secluded neighborhood around campus, nestled by trees and wooded areas.

When you entered the compound, your heart would be thrilled as you drove at an almost 45 degree uphill angle, on a spiraling driveway. That was always one of the most exciting things for me to do each time I returned home. I would come cruising up the driveway past the initial townhouses on both sides of the driveway, with the sound of sweet music radiating through my car's stereo speakers. It was as a dream always – truly a wonderful experience!

Driving halfway into the complex, you came to a four way intersection with a lovely patch of landscape in the center consisting of huge, beautiful limestone boulders. There was even a brand new pool and hot tub spa later added, that remarkably, was built just steps from my town home. The management could have chosen anywhere in that grand compound to build the pool and spa, however, The Lord caused them to choose my immediate, secluded area of the estate. I was so elated! It felt and looked as if I had a private pool and spa.

All the townhomes had a unique design to them. There was such architectural detail catered to each of the beautiful limestone homes. We had a barbecue grill and picnic area. We had a clubhouse. And we had spacious wooden private decks. You would see deer, bunny rabbits, and sometimes foxes running through the fields. My heart melted from the moment the leasing girl showed me the apartment.

Coming out of the heat of the hot summer's sun, and stepping onto the imported, tile entry floor, I was greeted by a fresh, ice cool breeze of central air conditioning that cooled my senses. There was no doubt that I had found my new home! I was in love! My new two story, two bedroom, two bathroom townhouse was simply amazing!

It had a grand contemporary wood burning fireplace. I had always dreamt of having my own authentic wood burning fireplace, and being able to watch movies and toast marshmallows as the flames roared with warmth. The dream that I had ever since I was a child, like many of my other dreams, was now a reality!

Blessings abound! My town home also had such dramatic 30' foot high ceilings, with brand new fresh scented tan carpets. The walls were a warm, off-white, cream-like color. I had a spacious gourmet kitchen with state-of-the-art appliances including an oven, range, dishwasher, and a refrigerator with an ice maker. My kitchen also had wonderful ceramic tile backsplashes. My kitchen had gorgeous countertops, and a washer and dryer in the pantry area. There was beautiful, custom-built, cherry cabinetry throughout the entire kitchen.

There were spacious walk-in closets in both the bedroom on the main floor, as well as the master bedroom upstairs. There were large windows that let much sunlight into my home and a sliding screen door in the living room that led to my spacious patio. I was now living in a serene paradise!

I had dreamt of living in The Boulders for the past few years. I used to drive by and get an amazing feeling of electricity in my chest, simply by looking at the gorgeous sprawling complex. It was a symbol of success. It was a symbol of achievement. It was a symbol of prosperity! I had also envisioned living there while I was living in the homeless shelter. No one thought that I would be able to live there. But I could see it so clearly, right there in front of me. And now, I was living in the dream! By the grace and power of Jesus Christ, soon, you too will be living in the dream!

Not only was I able to move into a huge 2 bedroom 2 bath, luxury townhouse apartment all for myself, but Christ caused the management to lease it to me, not for the normal $1,300 plus dollars that they charged other tenants, but for only about $500 dollars per month! The blessings were truly beginning to rain from the heavens onto me!

I must share this magnificent testimony, that only Christ could have architected. He was truly showing His son much favor on earth. I had been lifted and delivered within 60 days, from the depths of a homeless shelter, with absolutely nowhere to turn to, to then living in the president's home, and now, living in the most affluent, luxurious, and expensive, apartment complex around campus! Despite all my past sins and trespasses, Jesus Christ was showering me with abundant blessings, divine favor and wisdom!

Sometime before moving to The Boulders, I recall living with an awesome girl named Amelia. Amelia was the very first girl that I had ever lived with. I had met her a little over a year before. We were sexually intimate a few times during the year. In between my many relocations during that summer, she generously offered me a place to stay with her. I recall being so nervous about moving in with her. I recall asking all of my friends who had lived with a woman before, how their experiences were. They all had interesting and funny stories to tell. I decided to take a chance. It turned out to be quite an exciting and sexually charged experience. We had sex in the shower in the morning. We made love in the late hours of the night. We had long talks during the day. We connected on a deeper level. For the short time that I lived with her, that girl really helped me out a lot. I know she loved me with all her heart and would do anything for me. I will always hold Amelia dear to my heart. Wherever she is, she will always have my love.

Now, back in The Boulders, my private paradise on earth, I was ready to climb new heights during my upcoming fourth year in Bloomington, Indiana. Some days, when I opened the door with my keys, and looked at where I called home, I would have to pause and take it all in. It sometimes felt too good to be true.

Then one day, I noticed that I seemed to have had two of everything. I had two cars. I had two computers. I had two fairly big screen televisions in my living room. I had two video game consoles. I had two cell phones. Virtually everything that I had was two or more. I was well aware, however, that this was only the beginning, that The Lord had far greater plans for me.

As I had promised myself, I began taking biology, pre-med classes at Indiana University again. I did not worry about how I was going to pay or whether I was wasting my time. I was going to at least try. So once again, after two long years away from student life, every day, I went to my classes and studied at home. What an amazing feeling it was to be back! My spirits were certainly raised. My mind was clear. I was an Indiana University student again!

Chapter 29

Time raced by. Soon, it was October 7, 2004, the day that I had been waiting forever, since I arrived in Bloomington. It was my 21st birthday! It was an amazing time for me. As usual I had built up much anticipation, leading up to the date. I was the only one of my best friends who wasn't 21 years old yet. All of them had turned 21 during the previous school year. As usual, I was the baby in the group.

I recall that previous year being the most frustrating to
me. It seemed that I had managed to get into nightclubs and bars
fairly easily, from the time that I entered Indiana University at
the age of 17. However, when I turned 20 years old, the age
before the legal drinking age in the U.S., I was shut out of
nightclubs so many times, while my friends enjoyed themselves.
Now, I was turning 21 years old, finally!

That night had to have been one of the craziest nights I
had ever experienced in my many wild years in Bloomington. I
can't forget what I was wearing. I had on black boots, baggy
denim jeans, a throwback, Eric Dickerson, Los Angeles Rams,
football jersey, and a cone-shaped cardboard paper party hat that
matched the yellow, white, and baby blue colors of the jersey.
Needless to say, when they saw me, everyone knew that I was
the birthday boy.

I recall so many old college friends being so surprised
when I told them that it was my 21st birthday.

"Really Mike...!?" they would exclaim. "I thought
you've been getting inside the clubs since freshman year!"

I would smile.

Shot after shot of alcohol, drink after drink of beer,
friends and strangers kept buying me drinks. Beautiful women
were coming up to me, wishing me "happy birthday" and
locking lips with me. What a night! I wished every day was my
birthday!

In the following hours, I was in cloud nine! I must have
had over 20 drinks in my system! The mixture of music and
alcohol in my system was intoxicating. The next thing I know, I
wondered off away from my friends. I tend to do that a lot when
I'm intoxicated.

I floated my way down the street and around the corner
to another nightclub. I was in another world. The only thing I
remember was that I had arrived about an hour before the club
closed, and I was dancing and moving to the music, still with my
birthday party hat on, when out of nowhere, a woman, who must
have been in her late twenties to mid thirties, came up to me and
started dancing with me. I remember her body being in great
shape. We must have danced for less than a minute before we
began to kiss.

The next thing I know, she said, "I'm a doctor! Let's go home together!" Naturally, I became excited. I had never been with a doctor before. With much force, before I could even reply, she grabbed me by the wrist and pulled me out of the club. Her car, of course, was conveniently parked directly across the street from the club. We kissed aggressively in front of her car as she tried to open the door. She kept telling me how sexy I was. I would smile. I was just happy that I was going to have birthday sex.

When we got into her car, she was like a wild beast! She couldn't take her hands off of me. She asked me where I lived.

"The Boulders." I said.

She lived just a few blocks away from me.

Soon, we were speeding to my townhouse. We caressed, kissed, rubbed, and stroked one another during the entire ride. At every red light, the passion would intensify. It seemed that we could not get to my townhouse fast enough!

Finally, we arrived at The Boulders. When we rushed upstairs to my bedroom, we ripped each other's clothes off and began to have deep, passionate sex all night long! For hours, we were both in pure bliss. I will never forget how loudly she screamed and screamed the entire time. She scratched my back, continued to lose her mind, and screamed louder and louder! It felt as if the entire complex could hear her screams through my bedroom walls!

Suddenly, after hours of the doctor literally screaming my name at the top of her lungs as I penetrated in and out of her, I heard loud bangs downstairs at my apartment door! Could it be the Bloomington Police? Could they have been waiting for my 21st birthday to arrest me again? At that point, I would not put anything past them. Could this "doctor" really be an undercover cop?

Those thoughts quickly entered and exited my mind at the sound of the loud bangs on my door. But I was just too drunk to be too concerned. I attempted to get her off of me to check the door. But she tightened her pelvic muscles and just kept going!

"No Maubrey…!" she screamed in ecstasy, "Don't stop...!"

We ignored the door bangs, and continued to have sex in my luxurious apartment. As the seconds went by, the door bangs got louder and louder.

Finally, completely nude, in my "birthday suit", (no pun intended) with sweat dripping from my entire body, and a euphoric smile on my face, I ran down the stairs to see who was at my door.

Was it the police? No. Was it my friends, who I had wondered away from? No. It was my middle aged neighbor, who lived right across the walkway.

He yelled after I opened the door, "Can you guys keep it down!? It's 5 in the morning! I'm trying to sleep…!"

"I'm so sorry man." I said with the biggest smile on my face and an intoxicated glare in my eyes. "It's my 21st birthday..."

He could care less.

"Well keep it down!" he replied, and then stormed back across the walkway, back into his townhouse.

I could not believe that I made the doctor scream so loudly, that the sound of her voice traveled through the walls, almost 30 feet across the walkway outside my home, through my neighbor's walls, and into his bedroom.

After I had locked the door, I sprinted upstairs again, and proceeded to having wild, passionate sex with the doctor again. She struggled to keep from screaming the entire time.

I woke up the next morning, and had sex with her yet another time. This woman was like a cougar… like a beast! After our morning sex, she wanted to take me out for brunch for my birthday. I had already made plans, so I humbly declined. Besides, I was too exhausted to move. She went downstairs to get dressed, while I recovered from the long night in my bed upstairs.

Before I knew it, I could smell the scent of fried eggs coming from my kitchen downstairs. She was actually making me breakfast. I couldn't believe it. I was pleasantly surprised. I felt so special. I smiled as I gazed out the window, enjoying the scene of the beautiful morning. She came upstairs, wished me happy birthday, kissed me once more, and said goodbye.

"Wow! What a 21st birthday!" I thought to myself.

I relaxed in bed for some time after she left, then when I went downstairs, I was completely caught by surprise again. Next to the breakfast that she had prepared for me, was a crisp $20 dollar bill and her number written on a piece of paper.

"Wow!" I said with a hefty laugh.

I didn't know whether to feel special or to feel like a prostitute. What a 21st birthday! It was truly a night to remember!

Ironically, I decided to completely stop drinking alcohol the day after my 21st birthday. I had made the decision weeks before. You would think that after all those years of desiring to be able to buy alcohol and legally drink, that I would drink more often now that I had finally turned 21. But I was different. I was focused on my ultimate goal. Because I wasn't able to tryout for the Indiana University football team, due to lack of academic credits, I had made up my mind that instead of going through all the normal steps of reaching my goal of becoming a professional athlete, I was going to go straight to the source. I was going to train for hours a day virtually every day, all year long, then try out for the National Football League. I was going for the NFL!

It was a very ambitious goal, however I knew that I had the ability to do anything that I put my mind to. I had already proven that fact to myself many times over. There was nothing, nor no one that could convince me otherwise! A person of average faith would consider the fact that he was still facing 60 years in prison if convicted, and would dare not consider setting such high goals. However, I had no fear – no worries!

So, after four straight years of drinking at parties and nightclubs during the weekends, I had quit drinking completely. All my friends were surprised and confused as to why I decided to stop.

At first, they didn't think it would last long. Whenever someone offered me a drink during a night out, I would always humbly decline. They always asked me why, and oftentimes, thought that perhaps, I had had a bad experience with alcohol, or that I was a designated driver that night. I just told them that I was training for the NFL, and that I was focusing on keeping my body healthy. Most of my friends marveled with respect. I know now, from reading The Bible, that it is healthy and fine to drink in moderation, as long as you don't become drunk. However, it is amazing how things drastically change for the better when you don't drink.

Suddenly, one fateful night out in a sports bar, I was standing there by myself in the middle of the bar. My friends must have been upstairs dancing or socializing with women. I had on my usual pair of black boots, denim jeans, and a revealing tank top that highlighted my chiseled muscles. Out of nowhere, The Lord Jesus sent a man to me that changed the very course of my life toward a much more focused and positive direction.

Max Taylor! Max was an Indiana University student in his senior year that I had noticed over the course of the past few years in Bloomington. He was a mutual friend of an old freshman dormmate in Foster Harper. I can't remember our exact conversation, however I recall him approaching me, then us talking about my workout routine and my plans for trying out for the NFL. During our conversation, he told me that he was majoring in the health and fitness field, and would love to train me. It sounded like a good idea, but I honestly didn't think much of the offer.

All throughout my life, and especially in the recent months before that night, many friends and complete strangers would approach me, inquiring whether they could workout with me, and what my secrets were, in obtaining my physique.

Max and I exchanged cell phone numbers, but I did not contact him. My blissful and focused year was speeding by. It was now toward the end of December. All the students were going home for the almost month long winter recess. There was a huge snowstorm that had blanketed the town that week. I had saved up a few thousand dollars, and was in the middle of negotiating to buy my third car, in order to eventually sell months later.

The car was a fast, navy blue, Toyota Celica GT sports coupe. It was a stick shift, manual gear car. I had never driven a manual car in my life and had absolutely no idea how to operate one. I didn't care. The price was right, and I had to have it.

When I arrived at the dealership, I told the car dealer that I had no idea how to drive a manual car, but that I needed to drive to New Jersey the next day.

"No problem." he said. "I'll teach you. It's fairly simple..."

First, the dealer test drove the car, teaching me the basics, as I sat watching attentively in the passenger's seat for a few minutes. Finally, it was my turn! My heart raced as I exited the passenger's seat and walked around the car toward the driver's seat. So, in the snowy, slippery streets of Bloomington that cold afternoon, I got behind the wheel of the manual car, with the dealer sitting in the passenger's seat next to me, and I nervously began to drive. It was a very nerve racking experience. The car stalled out a few times, however, I understood the basics of driving the car.

After just a few minutes of the dealer teaching me, I finally exclaimed, "I'll buy it!" I obviously needed much more practice with a manual car, but I wanted the car badly, and I needed to drive home for Christmas. I paid thousands of dollars in cash for the car, signed the paperwork, and I was on my way! The car dealer must have thought that I was crazy!

I remember driving the car straight to my African friends' apartment complex. They were so excited to see the man they had watched live in a homeless shelter, just buy his third car. It was a celebration in that parking lot! I told them that I had just learned minutes ago to drive a manual car. They were shocked! I told them that I was going to drive it all the way home to New Jersey, the next morning. They too must have thought I was crazy.

"No problem... We can teach you..." they said.

They all knew how to drive a manual car. In many countries in Africa, manual cars are more predominant than automatic cars. With excitement, they test drove the fast Gt coupe that I had just bought. Later that night, with much snow still on the streets, my African brothers taught me how to drive the manual car.

Finally, about an hour of lessons later, I told them that I had learned enough. At that point, I knew that further lessons would not make me a better or worse driver during my upcoming journey, less than 12 hours away. That night, I recall staying up well past the late hours of the evening, listening to music and watching movies in my African friends' apartment.

Chapter 30

The next morning, with barely a few hours of sleep, I said a prayer, and put in the rapper, Eminem's brand new, recently released CD, 'Encore'. I turned the base and volume up, and set off from my private paradise cluster in The Boulders apartment complex, to my parents' new home, over 1000 kilometers away. I can feel the adrenaline and nerves that rushed throughout my entire body, as I made the first left turn out of the driveway, and into the snow covered street.

Because I had invested most of the cash that I had (as usual), I had limited gas and spending money – perhaps, a few hundred dollars. There was absolutely no room for error. There were no global positioning systems (GPS) in most cars at that time. I had nothing but handwritten directions, that I had copied from online, on a flimsy piece of white paper, the night before. If the directions would have flown out of the window, should I have decided to roll the window down at any point of the trip, I would have had a big problem. I would have risked getting lost, wasting much gas money and the possibility of being stranded in the middle of the country. Not to mention the fact that I was driving a manual car, halfway across the country with no insurance. My driver's license had also been previously suspended for not paying parking tickets!

Looking back now, I have no idea what was going through my mind. It makes me realize how bold, yet foolish I was. I had just learned to drive a manual car less than 12 hours prior. The mid-west had just been blanketed with a massive snowstorm. I had barely any sleep the night before. I had barely any money. My license was suspended. I had no insurance. And I had never driven more than two or three hours alone before. I was putting my life as well as the lives of others in serious danger. There were just countless things that could have went wrong along the trip, but I wasn't going to let anything stop me from seeing my family for Christmas!

It was a very interesting ride through the states. After my nerves calmed a few miles after driving, I became more comfortable driving in the higher gears. It was when I had to slow down in traffic, that the car stalled out a few times. But all together, I was driving fairly well for a person who had just learned how to drive manual the day before.

Hour after hour, I was getting closer to my family. Halfway home, I decided to play a joke on my mother and told her that, unfortunately, I wasn't going to be able to make it home for Christmas. I could feel her heart sink on the phone. I recall how sad she was that her baby was not coming home to see her for Christmas. I could tell by the tone of her voice, that she had been really looking forward and excited to seeing me. We finished talking, and I told her that I would make sure that I called her on Christmas day.

Meanwhile, into the night, I raced closer and closer to my loving family. Then, there I was, alone at the intersection of a back road late that night. There was a massive semi trailer truck to my distant left, barreling down the road in my direction! The truck was a good distance away, so I was sure that I could cross the intersection in time. I put the car in first gear, then gently released the clutch as I applied pressure to the accelerator pedal. I drove about 10 feet forward when the unthinkable happened! The car had stalled out on me! My heart sank! I panicked! Now, the speeding semi-truck was getting closer and closer to me. Its speed was not decreasing! Perhaps, the semi-truck driver hadn't noticed me stalled out in his path yet. I hurried to turn the car back on. I went about a foot forward, and then the car stalled again! I went into shock! My hands were shaking as I attempted to start the car again. The semi-truck driver, now only seconds from colliding into my car and ultimately ending my life, began honking his loud horn. It did not seem that he could slow the speeding truck down!

My tearful eyes, once again... They begin to water as I recall that life changing night. I took a final look to my left. I saw the bright beaming headlights as they raced closer to me. I saw my entire life flash before my very eyes. In a millisecond, I thought about my family, my friends, and all that I had been through in my life.

No...! It was not my time to go! Christ had much more in store for me. There was so much more for me to do in this lifetime! I turned the ignition one last time, and let The Lord take over my hands and feet.

221

I must pause once more, as tears overflow from my eyes. It was truly an emotional experience. Life changing! A true miracle had been performed by the hands of The Lord, Jesus Christ! Praise The Lord!

Just before the semi-truck collided into me, I was able to speed off, out of harm's way. Until recently, I had never told my family about that fateful night.

I continued forward on my journey. It was quite an experience driving through different states, into the night, all alone in that GT coupe. By then, I must have listened to that Eminem album over a million times. I had hardly any food in my system, and I was driving on only a few hours of sleep from the night before. By the time I had entered Pennsylvania, just a few hours away from my family, I began to hallucinate! My eyelids became heavier. Fatigue kicked in. I struggled to stay awake. Once again, I was foolishly putting my life in danger. I remember dozing off many times, then suddenly opening my eyes to the feel and sound of my tires vibrating on the ripples on the side of the road. I instantly realized that my eyes had been closed for many seconds. The Lord was certainly with me in that car.

The times that my eyes were open, it seemed that there were images of faces in the Pennsylvanian mountains ahead in the far distance. I really should have parked the car on the side of the road and gotten a couple of hours of rest. However, I did not want to risk a police officer pulling up behind my parked car and asking for my license and registration. My car would have been impounded, and I surely would have been arrested and taken to jail for driving with a suspended license and without insurance.

I pressed forward into the night. Then finally, after a long journey, through many states, through snow, sleet, and rain, I had arrived at the new town that my parents had just moved to – Belleville, New Jersey! However, the online directions were not accurate enough to lead me directly to my parents' house.

This was not good. For about an hour, now close to midnight, I drove around, circling the town of Belleville, asking anyone that I could see for directions to my parents' house. The street that my parents' home was located on was so secluded that most people had never even heard of it. And because I was driving at a much slower speed through the town, the manual transmission kept stalling out due to my inexperience.

I became more tired and frustrated as time went by. At any moment, I could be stopped by a police officer for not being able to drive safely on the road. Finally, I arrived at a grocery store's parking lot, carefully drove to a police officer who was parked on the lot, then asked him if he knew where my parents' address was.

"Sure. Follow me..." he said.

The officer was so kind and helpful that he offered to escort me to my parents' house. My palms sweated and my heart raced as I carefully drove behind the officer's car. Each stop sign and red light that we arrived at, my nerves climbed, as I attempted not to stall out. I had not traveled halfway across the entire country to be arrested and jailed just minutes from my parents' home.

At last, I had arrived at the house! I was so relieved! I thanked the police officer, wished him merry Christmas, and then parked my car in front of the house. I sat in the car for a few moments alone in the dark, under the midnight stars, reflecting on my journey and thanking The Lord for delivering me safely to my family.

I remember the huge smile on my brother's face when he opened the door. He was surprised to see that I actually came. We hugged and he helped me with my luggage. My mom was in her room fast asleep, and did not hear me knock the door. She speaks of how that night was one of the best Christmas surprises that she ever had. I quietly walked into her room, and gently shook her body to wake her up. Still half asleep, she opened her eyes and said "hello". And just as she was closing her eyes again, she took a second look at me and let out a loud burst of joy and happiness! At first glance, my mother had thought that I was my brother. Now, she realized that it was me! My joke, that I was not going to be able to come home for Christmas worked! My mom was absolutely ecstatic to see her son home for Christmas! We hugged and laughed for much time. It had been about a year since I had seen her. I am so blessed that I was able to make her day! Seeing the joy on her face certainly made my day!

Chapter 31

My wonderful stay with my family seemed to have flown by. Before I knew it, I was back in my beautiful town home at The Boulders, in college-town, Bloomington, Indiana. I was sitting in my living room watching a "Rocky" movie marathon, as the flames roared from my fireplace in front of me, when all of a sudden, I remembered Max Taylor, the student who wanted to train me. I was filled with a sudden surge of motivation! I had been given a vision from Above!

I wasted no time! I immediately scrolled down my contact list on my cell phone and gave him a call. He answered. I told him that if he still wanted to train me to prepare for the NFL, then I was definitely interested, and wanted to begin as soon as possible!

Every year, during spring time, there is an NFL tryout called the "NFL Combine" for men like me, who were not drafted by the NFL, or who did not play college football. It was early January, so in addition to the training that I had been doing on my own since living in the homeless shelter during the previous summer, I had an additional four or five months to train with Max and increase the intensity of my workouts.

I invited Max to my home for a meeting to talk about my seemingly impossible goals. Before he came, I had prepared all my goals in a notebook. As we read through my goals, he quickly realized that I wanted to break all the speed, quickness, agility, and strength world records. I was ready and willing to make the sacrifices, and work harder than I had ever done in my life. Max was 1000% percent with me! And that inspired and motivated me more! Max was a true believer! We had made a covenant. We were in agreement!

My new daily routine, in contrast to my previous jail and homeless shelter schedule consisted of: waking up at about 5am in the morning to eat a carbohydrate filled breakfast, usually a cinnamon raison bagel with some juice. That would take a few seconds. Half asleep, I would immediately go back upstairs and go back to sleep for about an hour or two before either going to the Indiana University student recreational center or biology laboratory class first, depending on the day of the week.

After that, I would come home and do homework or study for upcoming exams. Then I would drive right back to class, followed by my second workout in the Indiana University indoor track and field, which was with my new trainer, Max. We would meet at the same time, around 3pm every single weekday.

There was much blood, sweat, and tears during our workouts. I truly had never worked so hard, with such fire and love in my life! Max pushed me far and beyond my perceived physical limitations. Day after day, week after week, I sprinted and sprinted and sprinted! Through the cold winter days, I was getting bigger, faster, stronger, and more agile. I gave everything that I had on the track and field. There was not a day that went by that I wasn't completely exhausted after the training session.

Some days after training, I used to be so drained that I would tell Max to go on without me, as I laid on my back gasping for energy and air for long periods of time. Many times, I pushed my body so far that I vomited in the middle of my workouts. There was no stopping me! I was a man on a mission!

Soon, my vision of reaching the NFL became even clearer. My body was transforming into a work of art that I had never imagined. My mind was in harmony. My soul was in perfect balance. Each workout revealed to me who I really was, and why I was placed on the earth. Each workout humbled me and brought me closer to The Kingdom of Heaven! My life began to make more sense. Everything was coming into alignment. My friends could see a transformation in me. My posture was improving. People began to ask me if there was something different about me. Friends began to ask me whether I was getting taller. I exuded absolute confidence! My future seemed bright. All my cares and worries were given to Jesus. I was more focused than ever before!

Every morning, I woke up in my beautiful townhouse with tremendous excitement and music in the air. Every night, I slept like a prince. What a peaceful slumber! My days were pure and simple: eat, train, study, do business, and sleep. Sundays were my days of absolute rest and relaxation as I mentally prepared myself for the following week ahead.

227

It wasn't all work and no play, however. The secret, and what got me through the grueling weeks, was the fact that I celebrated on Saturdays with my friends and fellow school mates. And in my luxury townhome, I threw lavish champagne parties. I threw formal black and white parties. And I threw Hawaiian themed, luau parties. Those parties were one of my fondest memories. I always took my time and paid great attention to detail in order to create a sexy atmosphere during my themed parties. I bought the finest, most expensive drinks for my friends and guests, played the best music, had beautiful women at the parties, and kept the wood burning fireplace in my living room blazing under my 30' foot apartment ceiling.

When you walked into my home, you could smell the hypnotic aromas of French vanilla, lavender, apple cinnamon, and fresh roses. I always wanted to make it an experience that my guests would never forget. That is the perfectionist that has always been in me.

Stay with me now, as we flash forward, and travel into the future, exactly five years from that exact time period. We are now in the second week of January, in the year 2010. As I am writing this story to you, there has just been a devastating 7.0 earthquake that has just shaken the country of Haiti, ironically, the land where the recent love of my life, the woman whose sudden break up with me motivated me to write this book, is from. After all the numbers are counted, this event may be the most catastrophic natural disaster in recent human history! However, I sit here, writing with a peaceful calm, confidently assured about the simple truth of life, that from the moment our Lord, Jesus Christ died on the cross, we all won!

I understand that what the devil wanted to use for evil, shall be soon turned to good! This recent event also confirms and strengthens my notion that all we have to do is just keep giving and cheerfully believing! Surely, the wisdom is in the knowledge of The Truth!

Chapter 32

Now as we journey five years, back into the past, the year is 2005. The month is February. It is just days before February 14, Valentine's Day, the holiday of love, celebrated by many people throughout the world.

It is early in the evening. With the sound of the singer, Usher's CD playing heavily in my car stereo, I pulled up in my navy blue GT coupe, to one of the freshman dormitory buildings across the street from my former dormitory during my freshman year. I'm wearing a tank top, with my hair neatly trimmed, shaved, and curled into a stylish Mohawk. I see my brother waiting for me with his luggage in one hand. When he spots me, we exchange smiles. He shakes his head. This is his first time visiting me in Bloomington, Indiana. I had not seen him since my Christmas visit home. My brother gets into my coupe. We hug, and then we race off to The Boulders! He's excited to see the amazing place that I had been raving about for the past few months of living there. The Boulders!

The moment we entered the compounds of The Boulders, I could tell that he was impressed by the beauty. We raced up the winding driveway. We parked the car and walked to my front door. When the keys unlocked the door to my beautiful abode, and the music from my stereo system was ignited, a big smile came on his face. Nodding his head, I could tell that he was proud of me. He was proud of how far I had come! He was proud to see his younger brother doing well! My mom also, was scheduled to arrive at my home the next day. We were all excited to see each other in my new luxurious town home.

But, this was certainly not a casual, informal visit. After two long years, and three months, finally, my trial date was scheduled to begin in less than 48 hours! This was it! This was the moment that I had been preparing for!

It is quite an outer-worldly feeling to know that you are going to trial to face 60 years in prison, and that within days, all of the freedom that you had taken for granted for so many years could be stripped away with a jury's verdict and a loud bang of a judge's gavel.

Most, without the anointed Spirit of Christ, would be overwhelmed, frantically nervous, and more stressed than they had ever been in their lives. Not me!

My mom arrived the following day. As I had been from the beginning, and in the company of my mom and older brother, as we sat around the fireplace and television in my living room, I was confident, I was in harmony, I was cheerfully, I was mentally and spiritually focused! I could almost see the protective shield of Jesus Christ that surrounded my body!

I wonder exactly what was going through the minds of my mom and brother that night. I wonder what was going through the minds of all my friends and family around the world, as they anxiously anticipated my trial scheduled for the following morning.

That night, I recall asking my mom and brother to stay up with me, and watch Texas evangelical minister, Joel Osteen, preach on television. They agreed. I didn't tell them, but I wanted them to experience with me, for the first time, the man who had, without a doubt, been the most positive, encouraging, inspirational, motivational force in my life, throughout my entire criminal case! Joel seemed to have been sent by Jesus to deliver a special sermon just for me that fateful night before my trial. It was as if he was speaking directly to me. All the way from Houston, Texas, out of Joel's mouth, through the air waves, into my living room, through my eyes and ears, and into the depths of my soul, that evening, I graciously received The Spirit! I was fired up! I was re-energized! I was ready for the battle that lay just ahead!

Holding hands after Pastor Joel's sermon, we said a prayer and thanked The Lord for all of His blessings.

"You're going to shave your Mohawk before going to court tomorrow, right?" I recall my older brother and mom asking me.

"No," I replied confidently, "I'm going to keep it."

Immediately, a very worried and concerned look appeared on both of their faces. You would think that a 21 year old man facing 60 years in prison would shave his Mohawk before the first day of his trial. But not me.

My mom and brother proceeded to try to convince me that I should shave my Mohawk before going to trial. They even called my father in New Jersey and asked him to talk to me. Still, I was not willing to shave my Mohawk.

There was a moment that night that I briefly considered removing my Mohawk, but then, as I looked myself in the mirror, alone in my bathroom, I changed my mind. I was so sure and confident that I would walk into and out of the flames of the trial victoriously, that I knew in my heart that there was nothing that could change the course of what God had promised me. Not even a Mohawk.

My mind, as in the past, was set! The next morning, on Valentine's Day, February 14, 2005, was my moment of truth!

I woke up early, showered, dressed up neatly, with my collared shirt and tie, said a prayer with my mom and brother, and drove them to the Bloomington courthouse. It was a cloudy day with lightly drizzling rain coming from the heavens. We parked directly in front of the courthouse. Together as a family, we walked up the courthouse stairs, into the building, and through the metal detectors.

As I led my mother and brother up the stairs to my public defender's office, my mind was as clear as the view of a serene lake on cool autumn morning. I knocked, then gently turned the door knob and opened the door. We were greeted by the receptionist.

"Hi," I said humbly, "I'm here for my trial today. Can we go to Mr. Scott's Office?"

My public defender of the past two years was Wyatt Scott. That is the moment it happened! That's when the Lord and Savior, Jesus Christ's magnificent wonders, like the fulfillment of a glorious revelation, began to unfold! That's when the goodness of Heaven began to shake! I get instant chills throughout my entire body, as I write! The receptionist looked absolutely puzzled.

"That's odd... I don't have you on his schedule today."

Now, I was puzzled! I turned my head to my mom and brother. Their faces were puzzled too! The receptionist was puzzled. I was puzzled. My mom was puzzled. My brother was puzzled. Everyone was puzzled!

Exactly what was unfolding before our very eyes? The receptionist took a second and third look at my defender's scheduled appointments for the day.

"No... No, I don't have you scheduled for the day."

"Are you sure?" I asked perplexed.

I restated my full name.

"I'm sure." she replied. "Let me go to the back, and get Mr. Scott from his office."

While we waited, I thought, as had happened many times in the past two years, that the trial date was once again, continued to a future date. My family and I waited patiently.

"What are you doing here?!" my public defender said as he walked towards us.

"I'm here for my trial." I replied.

And with the same irritated, annoyed, and extremely busy look that he seemed to always have on his face, he shook his head from left to right.

"You didn't get the letter in the mail?"

"What letter?" I replied.

He seemed to have become even more irritated. He let out a laugh of annoyance, and shook his head once again.

"Follow me to my office!" he instructed us.

My brother, my mom, and I all looked at one another even more confused than ever. I didn't know what to think. When we got to his office, he shuffled through his desk and handed me some paperwork.

"Maubrey," he said, as he began to read the paperwork, "Your case has been dropped!"

My heart... It jumped! My chest... It warmed! Endorphins rushed throughout my entire body! I lifted my eyes from the paperwork and looked at my lawyer in the eyes. I turned to my mom and brother, who had flown over 1000 kilometers from New Jersey to a little town in Bloomington, Indiana to support me for my trial.

Their faces seemed to be in a sudden state of shock and surprise. Just like that; it happened so fast! The entire moment seemed just too surreal. It was as if all time was moving in slow motion...as if I had been in a movie for the past two years unknowingly, and that hidden cameras were going to come out of nowhere.

My brother and mom's eyes widened and retracted quickly. I could tell that they were thinking exactly what I was thinking. I could almost hear the sweet sounding heavenly angels singing in my head, and trumpets playing in the background.

I had passed the test of God! His face was shining brightly upon me! After almost two and a half years of immovable believing, after I had put every cell of faith into the Lord Jesus, after I had stood strong in what Christ was whispering into my heart, after so many opportunities to give up, give in, and concede to the suggestions and beliefs of my friends, family, and the world, the Lord said, "My son, now I know that you are a true believer in Me!"

God had softened the heart of the judge. God had softened the hearts of the prosecutors. And God had even softened the heart of my public defender, Wyatt Scott.

I am absolutely positive that the words to the prosecution and judge that came out of Mr. Scott's mouth over the course of the previous two years could have been completely different, if he was not pushed to fight for me.

I do recall one specific afternoon, just shortly before that day, as I sat in his office, he was advising me as usual, to take a probation plea. I continued to hold my ground.

And then he did something out of the ordinary. He left his office and brought in a woman that I had never seen before. He told me to explain once again to the woman and him, why I thought that I did not deserve to go to jail or get probation.

I was not prepared to give a speech, and I had no idea who this new woman was, but I started to speak. A few sentences into my testimony, I had felt something spiritual come into me that I had never felt before.

That afternoon in that office with my defender and the woman, my words seemed to suddenly flow seamlessly. I poured my heart out about how drastically the experience of getting arrested had completely reshaped and redirected the course of my life – how I was a new man. I spoke of how I had learned my lesson. I spoke of how I would never sell drugs again.

Although they knew and disapproved of me selling the legal herbals, I made them understand that through my various businesses, I was making a valiant effort to avoid ever selling illegal drugs again.

I let them know how much optimism and enthusiasm that I had for my future as a result of what I had learned from the trying experience that I was living through, day in and day out.

The room stood frozen, with all attention focused on me and the words that were coming from my tongue. My eyes watered as the emotion behind my words overwhelmed me. I spoke until I could not speak any more. I purged my soul with all that I had. The Lord was surely speaking through me.

When I finished speaking, they excused me, and I never saw that woman again. Now that I look back, I beg to ponder, whether that mysterious woman was a prosecutor or the district attorney, whether she wanted to hear for herself, and see with her own eyes, what man of such faith and confidence in the Lord would adamantly turn down a treasure chest of mere probation, in confident and unwavering expectancy of a sea of riches of complete freedom.

Perhaps, she had to see for herself, whether I was pure, whether I was a renewed and changed man. For now, I do not know the answer. What I do know is that the Lord Jesus Christ saved my life from the moment that I was arrested. He rained favor on me even from the beginning, when, out of many choices, He appointed to me the county's chief public defender, with the most influence, credentials, and knowledge, Wyatt Scott.

With my mom and brother to my side, I remember reading the paperwork that stated the reason for my case being dismissed.

It read: "...The State of Indiana has dismissed the case against Maubrey Okoe-Quansah for the pursuit of justice."

That phrase always seems to amaze me each time I think of it.

"For the pursuit of Justice..."

Amazing! If the definition of justice is: the quality of being just; righteousness, equitableness, or moral rightness, then the state of Indiana had made a sound decision in their pursuits!

I wasn't quite there yet, but after that two year journey, I was more righteous. I was more just. I was more moral.

I thanked Wyatt for all that he had done for me over the course of the past two years. We shook hands, and he gave me some encouraging words and advised me to continue to stay out of trouble.

I really appreciated all that he had done for me. My family and I said our final "Thank yous" and "Goodbyes", then left Wyatt's office and exited the courthouse.

When we entered my car, the rejoicing and celebration began! Everything still felt so surreal. The feeling was indescribable! Through the lightly drizzling rain, there was much hugs, smiles, kisses, music and praise on the ride back to my home.

It had to have been one of the happiest days of my life. I had witnessed and experienced a true life miracle! A miracle on Valentine's Day!

And ever since finding out that my case had been dismissed on February 14, 2005, every year, Valentine's Day has had an extra special meaning to me.

It was truly the day that Jesus showed His love for His son!

When we arrived at my town home, the celebration magnified! Music was in the air! There was dancing! There was jumping, rejoicing, and many more hugs! We popped bottles of champagne! I remember dancing on top of my bar countertop.

By then, the word of my great deliverance had spread rapidly. Cell phones began to ring continuously. Calls were coming in from my friends and family from all around the world!

We shared the celebration with my aunts and uncles from London. We shared the celebration with my family in Africa. The great news spread to New York and New Jersey. The news had spread to all my close friends on campus.

Everyone was so happy, and relieved especially, that I was now officially a free man.

But, on the contrary. I was a free man all along, from the moment I trusted in Christ!

We celebrated the victory with a big feast that my mom had prepared that afternoon, and then at night, my brother and I went over to my best friends' apartment to be with the amazing friends who had stuck by me the entire time.

Gavin, Landon, and Stella embraced and congratulated me as I walked through their door with my older brother. Still young and foolish, we chose to celebrate with drinks and marijuana. I felt that I needed the high after what I had been through for the past two years.

The next day, my family was gone. On the plane back to their normal lives they went, away from "The Maubrey Destined Movie" that I called reality.

Now, it was back to business again. I had been given a new lease on life! I spent the next few months left in the school year, training vigorously for the NFL supplemental combine. I increased my intensity, became even more focused, and eliminated distractions. It was now time to prepare for my destiny!

The Journey to The Kingdom of Heaven

.

The Maubrey Destined *Effect*

Vol. II

TO BE CONTINUED...

Special Thank You

First and foremost, I'd like to give thanks to The Lord and Savior, Jesus Christ for all that He has done for me and continues to do in my life. I'd also like to thank everyone who believed in me from the beginning. I thank everyone who has supported me from the beginning. I thank everyone who has encouraged me. Thank you all from the very bottom of my heart!

Sincerely,
Maubrey Destined

For *Exclusive* Photos, Videos, More Healing

&

Additional Books

Visit
http://www.maubreydestined.com

Add Me
http://www.facebook.com/maubrey

To:
Doha

Believe
Always!

SoBe
3/21/23

247